BEYOND THE SURFACE

DISCOVERING DEEPER PURPOSE

A Devotional Journey Through Ecclesiastes
for Teens and Young Adults

LENORA E TREMBATH

Beyond the Surface Copyright © 2025 by Lenora E. Trembath

All rights reserved. No part of this publication may be reproduced, distributed, or transmitted in any form or by any means, including photocopying, recording, or other electronic or mechanical methods, without the prior written permission of the publisher, except in the case of brief quotations embodied in critical reviews and certain other noncommercial uses permitted by copyright law.

Although the author and publisher have made every effort to ensure that the information in this book was correct at press time, the author and publisher do not assume and hereby disclaim any liability to any party for any loss, damage, or disruption caused by errors or omissions, whether such errors or omissions result from negligence, accident, or any other cause.

Adherence to all applicable laws and regulations, including international, federal, state, and local governing professional licensing, business practices, advertising, and all other aspects of doing business in the US, Canada, or any other jurisdiction, is the sole responsibility of the reader and consumer.

Neither the author nor the publisher assumes any responsibility or liability whatsoever on behalf of the consumer or reader of this material. Any perceived slight of any individual or organization is purely unintentional.

The resources in this book are provided for informational purposes only and should not be used to replace the specialized training and professional judgment of a health care or mental health care professional.

Neither the author nor the publisher can be held responsible for the use of the information provided within this book. Please always consult a trained professional before making any decision regarding treatment of yourself or others.

Unless otherwise indicated, all Scripture quotations are taken from The Holy Bible, New International Version® NIV® Copyright © 1973, 1978, 1984, 2011 by Biblica, Inc. Used with permission. All rights reserved worldwide.

Scripture quotations marked ESV are taken from the English Standard Version® (ESV®), copyright © 2001 by Crossway, a publishing ministry of Good News Publishers. ESV Text Edition: 2016. All rights reserved, published by Crossway Bibles, Wheaton, IL, U.S.A.

For more information, email thewisdomanswer@gmail.com.

ISBN: 979-8-9927877-0-2 (ebook)
ISBN: 979-8-9927877-1-9 (paperback)
ISBN: 979-8-9927877-2-6 (hardback)

OTHER BOOKS BY THE AUTHOR

The Wisdom Answer
Equipping Teens Living in a Culture of Deception
An Interactive Journal Based on Proverbs 1–9

COMING SOON IN 2025

Bible Wisdom for Tiny Hearts
A First Faith Coloring Adventure for Ages 3–5
Simple Stories, Big Love

Bible Wisdom for Little Hearts
A Faith-Building Coloring Adventure for Ages 4–7
Introducing Biblical Principles Through Art

Bible Wisdom for Growing Hearts
A Coloring Journey Through God's Word for Ages 6–10
Combining Faith, Creativity, and Character Development

GET YOUR FREE GIFT!

Unlock **eight** beautiful, reflective art pages designed to complement your journey through Ecclesiastes. Each page captures a key insight from each week's study, giving you an opportunity to reflect visually on what you're learning.

Request your FREE pdf copies at:

thewisdomanswer@gmail.com.

I'd love to see your journey unfold.

Feel free to share what you're learning from these lessons by tagging

@lenoratrembath on Instagram, or

The Wisdom Answer on Facebook.

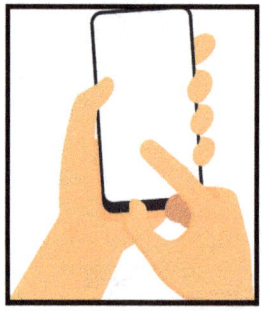

I dedicate this book to

my mom,

her sweet husband,

and my dad, looking down from heaven.

Table of Contents

Introduction
Why Ecclesiastes? 1

Week 1: When Empty Places Lead to Purpose 5

Day 1 - Finding Meaning 7
Day 2 - Purpose in Patterns 10
Day 3 - Original by Design 12
Day 4 - When the Path Isn't Clear 15
Day 5 - When Knowledge Weighs Heavy 17

Deep Dive: Week 1 Review—First Steps into Purpose 20

Week 2: Breaking Free from Empty Pursuits 23

Day 6 - When the Party's Over 25
Day 7 - The Achievement Trap 28
Day 8 - What We Really Hunger For 30
Day 9 - The Social Media Game 32
Day 10 - Why Keep Trying? 34

Deep Dive: Week 2 Review—Beyond Empty Pursuits 37

Week 3: Learning to Trust His Timing ... 39

Day 11 - Growing Pains ... 41
Day 12 - Right People, Right Season ... 44
Day 13 - The Gift of Today ... 47
Day 14 - Unfair ... 50
Day 15 - Beyond Now ... 53

Deep Dive: Week 3 Review—Trusting His Perfect Timing ... 55

Week 4: Growing Through Authentic Connection ... 57

Day 16 - When Others Hurt ... 59
Day 17 - Running Your Own Race ... 61
Day 18 - Breaking Free ... 64
Day 19 - Together We Stand ... 66
Day 20 - Unseen Wisdom ... 69

Deep Dive: Week 4 Review—Strength in Authentic Community ... 72

Week 5: Moving Past the Surface ... 75

Day 21 - Breaking Through the Noise ... 77
Day 22 - Vending Machine Prayers ... 79
Day 23 - Worth the Work ... 81
Day 24 - Finding Joy in the Journey ... 83
Day 25 - Reality Check ... 85

Deep Dive: Week 5 Review—Finding Joy in What's Real ... 87

Week 6: When Faith Gets Tested ... 89

Day 26 - When Life Hits Hard ... 91
Day 27 - Beyond Performance ... 93
Day 28 - When Heroes Fall ... 95
Day 29 - When Answers Aren't Enough ... 97
Day 30 - The Sweet Trap ... 99

Deep Dive: Week 6 Review—Finding Hope in Hard Places ... 101

Week 7: Wisdom for Life's Challenges 103

Day 31 - Facing Authority 105
Day 32 - When Control Slips Away 108
Day 33 - Into the Unknown 111
Day 34 - Love Worth Waiting For 113
Day 35 - Small Choices, Big Impact 116

Deep Dive: Week 7 Review—Choosing Wisdom in Daily Life 119

Week 8: Living for What Lasts 121

Day 36 - The Unexpected Power of Giving 123
Day 37 - Growing Through Light and Dark 125
Day 38 - More Than Skin Deep 128
Day 39 - Right Here, Right Now 131
Day 40 - Finding What Lasts 134

Deep Dive: Week 8 Review—Embracing Your Eternal Purpose 137

Next Steps - Moving Forward with Purpose 139
About the Author 143

Introduction
Why Ecclesiastes?

I'll be honest—when I first read Ecclesiastes, I thought it was depressing. Here was a book of the Bible repeating that "Everything is meaningless" over and over again. I couldn't understand how a man of Solomon's wisdom and accomplishments could conclude that life was this way.

But as I observed the world around me, I began to see the profound relevance of Solomon's ancient insights to our modern lives. We see it constantly in the entertainment industry—celebrities who achieve fame, fortune, and adoration, yet struggle with emptiness, addiction, or depression. Imagine someone today who has everything—career success, a beautiful home, a loving family—yet still feels unfulfilled. "I don't get it," they might say. "I should be happy, but something's missing." This common struggle resonates with so many of us. Think about it—why does this feeling of emptiness persist even when people have everything they thought they wanted?

That question led me back to Ecclesiastes, where Solomon wrestled with the very same struggle. As I dug deeper, something clicked.

The struggles Solomon wrestled with are exactly what so many of us face today:

- How do I find meaning when my career path feels uncertain?
- What defines my true worth when relationships keep disappointing?
- Where do I find purpose when my carefully planned future starts unraveling?
- Whom can I trust when even those I look up to fall? What I discovered changed my whole perspective on Ecclesiastes.

The word "meaningless," which Solomon uses 38 times, comes from the Hebrew word *hevel*—meaning vapor or smoke.[1] Like trying to grab smoke: you can see it, but it slips right through your fingers. It looks solid, yet it vanishes the moment you try to hold onto it. There's that initial excitement when something looks good, but that rush of satisfaction ends up fading faster than you expect. Like Solomon, you'll discover that achieving any earthly goal doesn't automatically bring lasting fulfillment.

You might ask, "Then, what does?"

As I studied his words, I noticed a phrase he kept repeating—one that unlocks the key to his realization.

Here's where Solomon's repeated phrase "under the sun" comes in—he uses it 58 times.[2] It describes living life focused solely on

---

[1] "Book of Ecclesiastes: Guide with Key Information and Resources," Book of Ecclesiastes | Guide with Key Information and Resources, accessed March 4, 2025, https://bibleproject.com/guides/book-of-ecclesiastes/.

[2] Gary Hamrick, "Cornerstonechapel," Cornerstonechapel.net, January 28, 2018, https://assets01.cornerstonechapel.net/documents/studyguides/20230129.pdf.

what we can see and achieve in this world rather than living connected to something bigger—connected to God.

Solomon lived both sides of this reality. Despite having everything our culture says should bring happiness—career success, relationships, wealth, influence—he still ended up feeling empty.

Through studying Ecclesiastes, I've found insights that speak straight to the heart of what you might be facing. This book will guide you on how to:

- Find authentic purpose when cultural values clash with spiritual ones.
- Build lasting relationships in a world of surface-level connections.
- Navigate both light and dark seasons with hope.
- Stay grounded when everything feels temporary.

I'd love for this to be more than just a study; I want it to be a conversation that continues beyond these pages. Throughout this devotional journey, I encourage you to reflect on your insights, questions, and how God is speaking to you. Many readers have found journaling their thoughts or discussing these principles in small groups brings additional clarity and deepens their experience.

My prayer is that through these eight weeks, you'll discover what Solomon learned the hard way: **life only feels meaningless when we chase temporary satisfaction.** With God, everything—even the career setbacks, the broken relationships, the uncertain seasons—becomes part of a bigger story.

I invite you to begin this journey, and may you discover the deep, unshakable purpose that only God can provide.

—Lenora E. Trembath

thewisdomanswer@gmail.com

WEEK 1

When Empty Places Lead to Purpose

Day 1
Finding Meaning

> *"The words of the Teacher, son of David, king in Jerusalem: 'Meaningless! Meaningless!' says the Teacher. 'Utterly meaningless! Everything is meaningless.'"*
>
> **—Ecclesiastes 1:1–2**

At first glance, Solomon's words sound extreme. How could everything be meaningless? But if you've ever felt like life's endless pursuits still leave you empty, his words might hit closer to home than you think.

Imagine having everything your social media feed says you should want: the picture-perfect life, dream relationship, fantastic career, and endless adventures—yet still feeling empty inside. It's like a phone battery that never stays charged. No matter how many times you reach 100 percent, you inevitably drain back to zero. You think, "This time, satisfaction will last," but it never does.

Proverbs 27:20 captures this perfectly: *"Death and destruction are never satisfied, and neither are human eyes."* We're wired to want more, convinced the next thing will finally bring fulfillment.

These pursuits aren't inherently wrong. The problem comes when temporary things become your source of meaning. Solomon's unsettling statement—"everything is meaningless"—isn't about despair; it's his wake-up call after discovering a profound truth: everything apart from God eventually disappoints.

Think about it: How many times have you reached a goal only to immediately start obsessing about the next one? This endless cycle isn't new to your generation—it's a human condition Solomon identified thousands of years ago. His journey through emptiness becomes our shortcut to discovering that true satisfaction isn't found in what we achieve, but in whom we know—the living God who brings meaning to everything else.

Key Point
Life gains meaning when lived in partnership with God.

Live It Out

- Write down one thing you're currently chasing (grades, followers, relationships). Instead of trying to want it less, ask: "How might pursuing this look different if I did it with God rather than for myself?"

- Reflect on this question: If a friend confided in you that they feel lost or like nothing really matters, what would you say?

- Find an image that represents meaning and purpose—maybe a sunrise, a path, or something symbolic—and share it with a friend, along with a reflection from today's reading.

Prayer

Lord, I confess I often seek meaning in achievements and approval. Draw my heart to You as my true source of purpose. Help me find worth in being Your child rather than in what I accomplish. Show me what it means to walk with You. Amen.

Day 2
Purpose in Patterns

"What has been will be again, what has been done will be done again; there is nothing new under the sun."

—**Ecclesiastes 1:9**

Have you ever felt like life is on repeat? You wake up, go to school or work, check your phone, and go to bed—only to do it all over again tomorrow. History itself seems to replay in endless cycles: empires rise and fall, societies wrestle with the same questions of justice and purpose—just as young people today seek their place in a complex world.

Like ocean currents reshaping a coastline, these repeating patterns mold our experiences, often in ways we don't immediately recognize. What seems like random repetition is actually God weaving His story through time.

If life is full of repetition, does that mean everything is meaningless? Not at all. Instead, these grand cycles reveal something profound about God's design. Across time, generations emerge and fade, yet an eternal pattern persists. These sweeping rhythms—from creation's first moments to everyday human experience—demonstrate how God orchestrates meaning beyond our understanding. As the psalmist declares, *"The plans of the Lord stand firm forever, the purposes of His heart through all generations"* (Psalm 33:11).

When we see life with an eternal perspective, these age-old rhythms take on fresh significance. Like currents shaping vast coastlines, our seemingly small roles contribute to God's grand design. Whether studying, working, creating, or serving, we participate in something beyond our immediate moment. Each action connects us to God's everlasting design, inviting us to see beyond the immediate and glimpse the profound interconnectedness of His ongoing work.

Key Point

In God's design, every pattern has purpose.

Live It Out

- Reflect on Patterns: Think about a pattern in your life—a recurring habit, challenge, or lesson. How might God be using it to shape you? Write your reflections and pray for wisdom to see His purpose in it.

- Learn from Others: Ask an older family member or mentor about a tradition they've carried throughout their life. What purpose have they found in this recurring practice?

- Share Your Insight: Share a meaningful pattern you've noticed—whether in nature, history, or your own life—with a friend.

Prayer

> *Lord, open my eyes to Your presence in these patterns. Help me see glimpses of Your greater plan. Reveal my place in Your divine purpose. Shape me through these sacred rhythms. Amen.*

Day 3
Original by Design

> *"'Look,' they say, 'here is something new!' But no, it has all been done long ago, before our time."*
>
> —Ecclesiastes 1:10

Ever heard someone say, "This is groundbreaking!" only to realize it's been done before? From fashion comebacks to ancient wellness practices resurfacing in modern health trends, the idea of "new" is often just recycled wisdom.

This verse challenges our notion of *new*. Fashion trends cycle back, scientific "discoveries" sometimes reveal ancient wisdom—like how fasting, long practiced in biblical times, is now recognized for its health benefits. Parents recognize timeless patterns as they watch their children navigate life's familiar milestones: first love, heartbreak, discovering their passion.

Each generation thinks they face unprecedented challenges—financial instability, political tensions, shifting values, social upheaval—yet the core human experiences of belonging, purpose, and identity remain unchanged across time. These repeating patterns might make life feel predictable, yet within these, God weaves something remarkable.

If nothing is truly new, does that mean our lives are just copies of the past? Not at all. Instead, within these repeating cycles, God does something extraordinary—He creates you!

Within these seemingly predetermined patterns emerges your unique design, like a fingerprint pressed into clay: you are God's original creation. *"I praise You because I am fearfully and wonderfully made; Your works are wonderful, I know that full well"* (Psalm 139:14). Even in "nothing new" activities, your personality, perspective, and purpose make each moment distinctly yours. You carry patterns that have never existed before and never will again.

Key Point

God creates originals, not copies.

Live It Out

- Think about one way God has made you unique—your personality, talents, perspective, or challenges that have shaped you. Write it down and thank God for how He designed you.

- Create something authentically you: Pick one:
  - Put together a playlist that reflects your story.
  - Take a photo that represents your uniqueness.
  - Write a short post about how God has shaped you.

- Share your creation with a friend or on social media.

Prayer

Lord, thank You for making me unique. In a world of endless cycles, You shaped me like no other. Help me make my own mark rather than pressing into old molds. Show me how to express the distinctive person You created me to be. Amen.

Day 4
When the Path Isn't Clear

"I applied myself to the understanding of wisdom, and also of madness and folly, but I learned that this, too, is a chasing after the wind."

—Ecclesiastes 1:17

Your to-do list is endless. Classes. Career paths. Job applications. Three activities on the same day? Your church bulletin lists ministry teams needing help. Each option seems to call, "Choose me," while your mind races: *"What do I do? What if I mess this up? What if I miss out?"*

So we do what seems logical—we make pros/cons lists. We text friends for advice. We scroll through reviews. We try to predict every outcome before taking a step. But with each opinion, clarity remains elusive.

Even with careful planning, sometimes the answer still feels unclear. That's when God invites us to stop striving and start trusting.

Here's God's command: *"Trust in the LORD with all your heart and lean not on your own understanding"* (Proverbs 3:5).

Think of your phone's GPS. When you take a wrong turn, it simply says, "Recalculating," and finds a new route. Sometimes, the detour shows you views you'd have missed on the *"perfect"* path.

God's guidance works similarly. He's less concerned with your perfect plan and more interested in your daily trust. Each "recalculating" moment is an opportunity to lean into His wisdom. Your path may twist unexpectedly. But real peace comes when you don't need to see every turn ahead—you just trust the Navigator who walks with you.

Key Point

Your journey with God matters more than mapping a perfect plan.

Live It Out

- Think about a decision you're struggling with now. Write it down and pray, asking, "Lord, which direction would You have me go?" Instead of trying to figure out every detail, ask, "What's the next right step I can take in faith?"

- Take action:
  - Text a mentor and ask them to pray for wisdom with you.
  - Find a verse about God's guidance and write it somewhere you'll see it daily.
  - Take a quiet moment to listen for God's direction, then share a reflection from today's reading with a friend.

Prayer

Lord, when I'm tempted to chart my course alone, help me find peace in following You. Guide my steps not toward perfection, but toward deeper trust in Your direction. Show me that Your presence matters more than my perfect plan. Amen.

Day 5
When Knowledge Weighs Heavy

"For with much wisdom comes much sorrow; the more knowledge, the more grief."

—**Ecclesiastes 1:18**

The weight of knowledge is real. A struggling friend's text, another heartbreaking headline in your feed, a younger sibling's concerning choices. You tell yourself not to overthink it, but the heaviness lingers.

Like gathering storm clouds, each piece of information adds weight, making everything feel overwhelming. We try to stay informed, to care, to make sense of it all. But the more we know, the more helpless we can feel.

We scroll, we study, we learn—and sometimes wish we could unlearn. A documentary about suffering leaves us wrestling with difficult questions. Even within our church families, prayer requests reveal layers of pain we never knew existed. Knowledge that should enlighten us often leaves us feeling small and helpless.

But God doesn't just offer information—He transforms what we know into wisdom that moves us toward action.

When that documentary haunts you, He helps you recognize injustice in your own community. When statistics about youth depression overwhelm you, He shows you how to truly listen when a friend reaches out at 2 a.m. Through His wisdom, overwhelming facts become fuel for practical love. *"If any of you lacks wisdom, you should ask God, who gives generously to all without finding fault"* (James 1:5).

Key Point
When knowledge weighs heavy, God's wisdom gives strength to carry it.

Live It Out

- Identify and Reflect: Take a deep breath and acknowledge what's weighing on you today. Choose one heavy piece of knowledge—a difficult truth, a news story, or a friend's struggle. Write it down.

- Pray and Invite God: Pray over what you've written, asking God for wisdom in how to respond. Instead of carrying the weight alone, invite God into it. "God, what do You want me to understand from this?"

- Apply and Share: List three ways this knowledge could make you more effective in serving others. Find a Bible verse about wisdom or peace as a reminder that God carries the burden with you. Share your insights with a trusted friend or mentor.

- Wisdom isn't just knowing more—it's knowing what to do with it.

Prayer

Lord, in this flood of information, be my shelter. Transform what overwhelms me into wisdom that serves others. Help me see beyond the facts to the faces of those I can help. Guide me from confusion into Your peace. Amen.

Deep Dive: Week 1 Review
First Steps into Purpose

As this first week concludes, consider how your understanding of purpose has evolved. Solomon discovered what we're exploring—true meaning comes not from worldly pursuits but from walking daily with God. This journey isn't just about finding answers—it's about discovering who you were created to be in relationship with your Creator.

Pause and Reflect

1. Which day's message resonates most with your current struggles? How does its core truth address what you're facing?

2. Review your Live It Out responses from the week. What patterns do you notice about where you've been looking for meaning, validation, or certainty?

3. This week used several metaphors. Which one helped you understand God's role in your life more clearly? Why?

Creative Expression

Capture your growth this week in one of these ways:

- Create a visual showing what drains your life's battery versus what truly recharges you in God.

- Document a pattern in your life and reflect on how you now see God's purpose within it.

- Design a symbol that represents your unique place in God's greater story.

Truth to Remember

God transforms what feels empty into what has eternal purpose. In relationship with Him, every pattern, decision, and piece of knowledge finds its meaning.

Looking Ahead: Breaking Free from Empty Pursuits

With our foundation set—purpose found in God, not worldly pursuits—it's time to break free from the distractions and false promises that keep us stuck. **Week 2** will challenge us to examine where we've been placing our trust and what it looks like to truly let go of the things that drain us. We'll explore themes of identity, comparison, and the temptation to seek fulfillment in temporary things.

Get ready—this next week is all about freedom.

WEEK 2

Breaking Free from Empty Pursuits

Day 6
When the Party's Over

> *"I said to myself, 'Come now, I will test you with pleasure to find out what is good.' But that also proved to be meaningless ... And what does pleasure accomplish?"*
>
> —**Ecclesiastes 2:1–2**

The music pulses through the room, lights flashing with the rhythm. Someone snaps a picture—capturing the moment, freezing the illusion. Maybe it's not a party for you but hours lost gaming or scrolling until your eyes blur. It feels good. Until it doesn't.

Pleasure comes in many forms—thrilling parties, binge-watching shows, seeking validation through likes. All promising escape. That next level, that viral moment, that rush that might finally satisfy.

But does it ever?

It's like drinking saltwater when you are desperately thirsty—each sip makes you thirstier. "Just this once. Just one more." The promise of fulfillment feels real, yet every high requires a bigger one next time. And in the end, every pursuit apart from God leaves you emptier than before.

What are we really chasing? The party, the thrill, the escape—they all hint at something deeper: a longing for joy, purpose, connection. But they can't deliver what only God can.

Jesus promises, *"Whoever drinks the water I give them will never thirst. Indeed, the water I give them will become in them a spring of water welling up to eternal life"* (John 4:14).

True satisfaction isn't found in the temporary highs—it's found in the presence of the One who created you. It's in quiet moments in His Word, honest conversations, and friendships where you're fully known. These aren't quick fixes; they are deep wells of living water that never run dry.

Key Point
Empty pleasures leave us thirsty; Jesus alone satisfies.

Live It Out
- Reflect on these questions:
  - What do you use to escape or find quick satisfaction?
  - What deeper need lies underneath?
  - Are you craving connection, purpose, rest?

- Write down two ways to redirect that longing toward fulfillment. Maybe it's reaching out to a friend for a real conversation instead of scrolling. Choose one to commit to this week.

- If a friend felt empty, what truth from today would you share? Write it as a text message, then send it

Prayer

Lord, when temporary pleasures tempt me, draw me to Your living water. In emptiness, help me remember that You alone quench my deepest thirsts. Let Your presence refresh me and Your joy flow through me. Guide me toward what truly satisfies. Amen.

Day 7
The Achievement Trap

> *"I undertook great projects ... I became greater by far than anyone before me ... Yet when I surveyed all my hands had done, everything was meaningless."*
>
> —**Ecclesiastes 2:4,9,11**

The drive to achieve is everywhere. Marcus pours hours into robotics competitions, each victory pushing him toward another. Sarah's art earns recognition, yet success demands more. Like climbing an endless ladder, every step reveals another rung. With each milestone, doubts linger: *Will this be enough? What if I fail?*

These efforts aren't bad—they're glimpses of God's gifts. Hard work, skill, and perseverance are valuable. But what happens when the trophy gathers dust? When the art gallery grows quiet? When the applause fades, and the familiar emptiness creeps in? Achievement becomes just a checkmark, leaving us wondering why success feels so unsatisfying.

"The Lord does not look at the things people look at. People look at the outward appearance, but the Lord looks at the heart" (1 Samuel 16:7). While the world sees accomplishments, God sees deeper—every effort, setback, and moment of perseverance. He isn't measuring your worth by how much you achieve, but by the heart being formed through the journey.

Your value doesn't rest in awards or titles. It's unshakable because it's based on who you are in Christ. He created you for more than the pursuit of endless achievements—He created you to live in the security of His love, knowing that even when the applause stops, you are still His.

Key Point
Your worth is found in who you are, not in what you achieve.

Live It Out
- Take a few minutes to reflect and write two lists:
    - **What I Do:** List your accomplishments and talents.
    - **Who I Am:** Write down your God-given identity and how your gifts can serve others.

- Choose one way to use your talents to help someone this week. Maybe it's tutoring a friend, creating something meaningful, or offering encouragement to someone struggling.

- Thank someone you admire not just for achievements, but for their character.

Prayer

> *Lord, thank You for the gifts and talents You've given me. When I'm tempted to measure my worth by achievements, remind me that You see beyond trophies and recognition. You see my heart. Help me rest in the truth that my identity is secure in You, not in what I accomplish. Use my gifts to honor You and serve others. Amen.*

Day 8
What We Really Hunger For

> *"I denied myself nothing my eyes desired; I refused my heart no pleasure ... Yet when I surveyed all that my hands had done and what I had toiled to achieve, everything was meaningless."*
>
> **—Ecclesiastes 2:10–11**

You know the feeling —the rush when you finally get what you've been wanting. Maybe it's the newest phone, the perfect outfit, or an upgrade that promises to change everything. For a moment, anticipation turns to satisfaction. But weeks later, the feeling fades. The phone is just a device, the outfit loses its appeal, and craving for the next best thing creeps in. What once seemed essential now sits forgotten.

Like a traveler spotting water in the desert, we chase mirages of fulfillment—trendy clothes, social media likes, success. But when we reach them, we grasp at sand. No matter how much we consume, the hunger never disappears.

"Why spend money on what is not bread, and your labor on what does not satisfy? Listen, listen to me, and eat what is good, and you will delight in the richest of fare" (Isaiah 55:2). Behind every worldly craving is a spiritual hunger—a longing for purpose, love, and iden-

tity. The things we chase aren't bad in themselves, but they can't nourish the soul.

The constant craving for more? It's not because we desire too much—but because we settle for too little. God offers something better: true satisfaction in Him. A feast that never leaves us empty.

Key Point
Your deepest wants are pointing to your greatest need—God.

Live It Out
- Take a moment to reflect: What are you really craving?
  - Is it belonging? Are you chasing approval through social media or popularity?
  - Is it security? Are you clinging to achievements or material things?
  - Is it love? Are you looking for relationships to define your worth?
- Choose one area where you've been searching for fulfillment in temporary things. Instead of chasing the next "fix," spend time with God—read Scripture, journal your thoughts, or talk to a friend about how real fulfillment comes from Him.

Prayer

Lord, when I feel restless, remind me that no possession, achievement, or relationship can truly satisfy me—only You can. Help me see past the illusions of fulfillment and reach for Your lasting nourishment. Teach me to delight in the richest fare that comes from knowing You. Amen.

Day 9
The Social Media Game

> *"Then I considered all that my hands had done ... and behold, all was vanity and a striving after wind, and there was nothing to be gained under the sun."*
>
> —**Ecclesiastes 2:11**

Another selfie. Another edit. A new angle. The lighting's almost right, but your arm looks weird. Delete. Retake. Filter. The caption has to be clever—not too try-hard. Minutes pass. Finally, you post. And now, the waiting begins.

At first, likes and comments feel thrilling. Validation. Then, scrolling takes over. A classmate's perfect vacation shot. Friends hanging out without you. An influencer's effortlessly amazing life. Your joy shrinks into the background.

Like an actor trapped in an endless performance, we carefully stage, adjust, and perfect—curating a highlight reel of smiles, achievements, and adventure. But behind the scenes? The exhaustion of thirty deleted photos, the pressure of keeping up, the weight of wearing a mask that never fully comes off.

Mia knew this cycle. She spent an hour crafting the perfect beach photo—tweaking angles, smoothing lighting, choosing poses. The flood of likes felt like applause. But soon, someone else's post outshined hers—a tropical vacation, a new relationship, a more exciting life. The familiar ache whispered: *You're not enough.*

While followers see the character we've created, God sees something deeper. *"You desire truth in the inward being"* (Psalm 51:6). He's not impressed by filters or highlight reels. He's drawn to the heart behind the posts, the real person. While the world claps for performance, God cherishes the person behind the curtain—flaws and all.

Key Point
The authentic you is more powerful than any role you could play.

Live It Out
- Take a real moment to step off the stage today:
    - Look at your last post. What was happening outside the frame? Were you happy, or were you just trying to look happy?
    - Post something real—an ordinary moment, an honest thought, a small joy that doesn't need a filter.
    - Or try a 24-hour break from social media. Instead of scrolling, text a friend, go outside, or journal what you're really feeling.

Prayer

> *Lord, I'm tired of this endless performance. I don't want to live for likes or approval. Help me step away from the pressure to be perfect online and into the freedom of being fully known and loved by You. Give me the courage to be real today—no filters, no masks, just who You created me to be. Amen.*

Day 10
Why Keep Trying?

"What do people get for all the toil and anxious striving with which they labor under the sun? ... Even at night their minds do not rest."

—**Ecclesiastes 2:22–23**

It's 2 a.m. Your eyes burn from staring at the screen. The assignment is due tomorrow. You were supposed to start earlier, but now you're here—too wired to sleep, too drained to focus.

A notification flashes. Your mind spins—*What if I fail? What if I fall behind?* You open TikTok, but the comparison trap tightens—someone else seems more productive. Sleep? That's just lost time you could be using to catch up.

Like hamsters on a wheel, we keep running. Five more minutes studying. Another energy drink. The faster we go, the further behind we feel. If we just grind harder ... *it'll* be enough. But the wheel never stops.

Then, Jesus speaks: *"Come to me, all you who are weary and burdened, and I will give you rest"* (Matthew 11:28).

This isn't just permission for a break—it's an invitation off the wheel. Your worth isn't measured by your GPA or followers. God offers a different way beyond endless striving.

In His presence, you can breathe. You're already enough because you belong to Him. When you no longer have to run to prove your worth, you can pour yourself into life without fear.

- Instead of pulling an all-nighter out of fear, you study because you want to learn.
- Instead of posting for validation, you share because you want to connect.
- Instead of measuring yourself by achievements, you find peace in God's love—secure and unearned.

One path is driven by fear. The other by *freedom*.

Key Point

Your worth rests in *Whose* you are, not how well you perform—that's why you can freely give your best.

Live It Out

- Take a real step toward rest today:
  - Identify moments this week where you felt pressure to keep running.
  - Write how these situations change when approached from God's love, not fear.
  - Tonight, surrender one anxiety to God and set a boundary— log off earlier, say no to one task, or pause before reacting.

Prayer

Lord, when tempted to keep running on this endless wheel, help me step into Your rest. Let me find peace in Your unchanging love, not in perfect performance. Give me wisdom to work hard, courage to stop, and faith to trust I don't have to earn Your love. Amen.

Deep Dive: Week 2 Review
Beyond Empty Pursuits

As Solomon discovered, our world's constant chase for more—temporary highs, achievement, material things, social approval—ultimately leaves us feeling empty, a truth we examined this past week.

God never intended for us to live in a cycle of proving or performing. What if peace comes not from achieving more, but *trusting* more? The more we grasp for things that don't last, the more drained we become—but when we release control to God, we find the deep rest our souls crave.

Pause and Reflect

1. Which empty pursuit resonates most with you—temporary highs, achievement, material possessions, image maintenance, or proving your worth? What makes God's rest seem so elusive?
2. Review your **Live It Out** from this week. What patterns emerge about what you're trying to prove and why?
3. Of this week's metaphors, which most vividly captures your struggle? Why?

Creative Expression

Express your journey beyond empty pursuits in one of these ways:

- Create a visual that contrasts what gives lasting satisfaction versus what only provides temporary relief.

- Journal about how you are growing in ways that truly matter rather than just achieving things that fade.

- Write a letter to your future self about where you seek genuine peace.

Truth to Remember

Your worth isn't found in what you chase or achieve—it's already secure in *Whose* you are. In God's presence, you're free to both rest and give your best without proving your value.

Looking Ahead: Learning to Trust His Timing

This week, we learned that chasing the wrong things will always leave us empty. But what happens when God's timing doesn't match ours? **Week 3** will challenge us to examine how we handle waiting, delays, and uncertain seasons. It's easy to trust God when life moves forward—but what about when He says, "Wait"?

Get ready—this next week is about learning to rest in God's perfect timing.

WEEK 3

Learning to Trust His Timing

Day 11
Growing Pains

"There is a time for everything, and a season for every activity under the heavens: a time to be born and a time to die, a time to plant and a time to uproot..."

—Ecclesiastes 3:1–2

The text message comes through: *Hey, I think I'm gonna start sitting with Jamie at lunch.* You stare at the screen, a knot forming. This was your person—who knew your jokes, your late-night thoughts, your "safe space." Just like that, something shifts.

Maybe it's a friendship changing. Maybe it's doubting your faith. Or your planned future suddenly feels impossible. Like a plant pushing through hardened soil, change stretches us, even painfully.

Growth isn't constant. Some days, a new leaf unfurls. On other days, nothing visible happens. But beneath the surface, roots stretch deeper, preparing for what comes next.

Your life follows this same pattern.

- Your friend gets their driver's license on their first try; you're still stuck practicing in empty lots.

- Someone else has a clear career path; yours is a maze of uncertainty.

- Their faith looks unshakable; yours has questions.
- Invisible growth is still growth.

God transplants your life—through friendship shifts, faith questions, or uncertain paths—it's not to harm you, but to cultivate something more meaningful within you.

The God who turns winter into spring is tending your heart. Even in waiting, He works: "Being *confident of this, that he who began a good work in you will carry it on to completion*" (Philippians 1:6).

What feels like a setback is preparation. What looks like loss is often making space for something new. He's still planting, pruning, and growing something in you.

Key Point
When God plants or uproots, His purpose is always your thriving.

Live It Out
- Identify one growing pain you're facing—a friendship change, family conflict, or faith question. Write it down, then reflect:
    - What strength might God be developing in me through this?
    - Where do I see God's presence, even subtly?
    - What small step can I take to grow, not just survive?
- Plant something small this week—even just a seed in a cup. Let it remind you: growth is happening, even when you can't see it yet.

Prayer

Jesus, I'm struggling with _____. When this hurts, remind me You're not wasting my pain. Help me trust the growth beneath the surface. Thank You for cultivating who I'm becoming and deepening my roots in You. Show me how to trust through this change. Amen.

Day 12
Right People, Right Season

"A time to embrace and a time to refrain from embracing, a time to keep and a time to throw away."

—Ecclesiastes 3:5–6

Your phone buzzes. *Hey, you up?* A name flashes across the screen, and something in your chest tightens. Maybe it's the friend who only texts when they need something. Maybe it's someone who pulls you into habits you regret. Or maybe it's someone who once brought joy—but now leaves you feeling drained.

Then there are the other names—the ones that make you smile before you even read the message. Friends who notice when you're off, who speak hard truths, who show up, even when it's inconvenient.

"Wounds from a friend can be trusted, but an enemy multiplies kisses" (Proverbs 27:6). True friends don't just echo what you want to hear—they care enough to speak up when they see you slipping.

Think of your heart like a backpack with limited space. Some friendships make you stronger for the road ahead. Others weigh you down, leaving you exhausted.

- Maybe it's a friendship that used to be good but now holds you back.

- Maybe it's a relationship that constantly crosses boundaries.

- Maybe it's someone you keep trying to fix—but they aren't ready to change.

- If you hold on to what's not meant to stay, even small hills feel like mountains. What if releasing the weight isn't loss—but preparation for healthier, stronger relationships?

Key Point

Healthy relationships require courage—to embrace the right ones and release the rest.

Live It Out

- Examine your three most recent conversations and ask:
  1. Do I feel more authentic around this person?
  2. Are they drawing me toward or away from God?
  3. What action do I need to take—setting boundaries, having an honest conversation, or investing more?

- Now act:
  - Thank a friend who lifts you up.
  - Set a boundary with someone who drains you.
  - Pray about a friendship in the gray area.

- **Friendship isn't passive.** Who needs to hear this today? A friend struggling with a toxic relationship? Someone needing encouragement to invest in deeper friendships? Reach out and encourage them today.

Prayer

God, when I consider my closest friendships, especially _____, I need Your wisdom. Show me which relationships to invest in and which need distance. Give me courage for difficult conversations, strength for boundaries, and wisdom to choose friendships that help me choose You. Amen.

Day 13
The Gift of Today

"He has made everything beautiful in its time. He has also set eternity in the human heart; yet no one can fathom what God has done from beginning to end."

—Ecclesiastes 3:11

You rush through the day—scrolling between tasks, flipping between notifications, glancing at conversations but not really hearing them. By evening, it's all a blur. You were *busy*, but you can't remember anything truly meaningful.

How often do we rush past what God is making beautiful right now?

Solomon saw it, too—how easy it is to miss what matters most. We race through life, filling every second, while eternity whispers in the background.

"See, I am doing a new thing! Now it springs up; do you not perceive it?" (Isaiah 43:19).

- That conversation between classes or at work? It might change someone's day.

- That seemingly endless assignment? It's shaping you in ways you don't realize.

- That moment when you feel the urge to check your phone? God is waiting to speak.

But we don't notice—because we're already thinking about what's next.

That restlessness in your heart—the one that makes it hard to slow down? It's not just busyness. It's your soul longing for something deeper.

God placed eternity in your heart, not endless activity. While anxiety tells you to keep moving, God invites you to pause. His beauty isn't found in constant motion, but in moments where you let His peace settle like fresh snow—transforming rushing into rest.

Key Point
Even in ordinary moments, God is creating beauty—if we slow down enough to see it.

Live It Out
- Set three alarms on your phone at random times today. When each goes off, pause for thirty seconds and notice one beautiful thing God is doing at that exact moment:
  - Maybe it's the kindness in someone's voice
  - Maybe it's sunlight spilling through a window
  - Maybe it's just the gift of breathing in a quiet moment
- Write these moments down. At the end of the day, reflect:
  - How did pausing change my perspective?
  - What moments would I have missed if I hadn't stopped to see them?

Prayer

God, my heart is always racing to the next thing, but You've placed eternity within me—not to make me restless, but to draw me closer. Open my eyes to see Your beauty in today's ordinary moments—especially in _____ (name a specific situation). Transform my rushing into rest as I learn to be fully present with You. Amen.

Day 14
Unfair

> *"I saw something else under the sun: In the place of judgment—wickedness was there, in the place of justice—wickedness was there."*
>
> **—Ecclesiastes 3:16**

You put in the effort. You told the truth. You did the right thing.

Yet, someone else gets the credit or the reward. Meanwhile, you're left cleaning up the mess, taking the blame, or watching the wrong person win. The frustration of injustice knots up inside you.

Life feels like a rigged game sometimes. The liar gets believed, the cheater moves forward. You play fair, but the scoreboard says you're losing.

Jesus doesn't sugarcoat it: *"In this world you will have trouble."* But He continues: *"But take heart! I have overcome the world"* (John 16:33).

God sees every move:

- Joseph—framed and forgotten in prison.

- Daniel—thrown to lions for his faith.

- Jesus—standing trial while the truth got twisted.

False accusations didn't stop their stories—and they won't stop yours.

Unfair situations test what's inside you. Will bitterness take over? Or will character shape your choices?

Life's outcome isn't decided by who gets ahead today, but by how you respond when things aren't fair. God sees beyond this moment. Your worth isn't defined by someone else's misled opinion. What feels like a dead end is strengthening you in ways you can't see yet.

Key Point

Choose what's right today, and watch how God uses it for something greater tomorrow.

Live It Out

- Think about one unfair situation you're facing right now. Ask yourself:
  - What's the easiest response? (Getting even? Giving up?)
  - What's the response that reflects the person I want to become?
  - What's one action I can take today toward integrity instead of resentment?
- Encourage someone else today. Chances are, you're not the only one feeling like life is unfair right now. Send a message, share this devotional, or remind someone that God sees what others miss.

Prayer

God, this feels so unfair right now. When I want to give up or get even, remind me that You see the bigger picture. Help me respond with strength, not bitterness. When the game feels rigged, remind me that Your justice never fails. Transform this moment into something good in my life. Amen.

Day 15
Beyond Now

> *"All go to the same place; all come from dust, and to dust all return. Who knows if the human spirit rises upward?"*
>
> **—Ecclesiastes 3:20–21**

Grief doesn't follow a script. One moment, you're okay; the next, a memory blindsides you. A song they loved plays, and the ache returns. You reach for your phone before remembering—they're gone. Their empty seat, their favorite hoodie that still smells like them, old messages—fragile threads to someone who's no longer here.

The world offers empty platitudes like *"They're in a better place"* or *"Time heals everything,"* but they fall short. Loss doesn't just fade. It lingers, reshaping how we see life, time, and the people still around us.

Rich or poor, famous or unknown, we all face the same questions:

- Is this really all there is?

- What happens next?

- Will I ever see them again?

Yet, in our grief, God speaks. Paul writes, *"We believe that Jesus died and rose again, and so we believe that God will bring with Jesus those who have fallen asleep"* (1 Thessalonians 4:14). Jesus Himself promises, *"I am the resurrection and the life. The one who believes in me will live, even though they die"* (John 11:25).

These aren't just comforting words—they're declarations of hope. They remind us that in Christ, death is not the end of the story.

Key Point

In Christ, loss is not forever. Death is not the final chapter.

Live It Out

- Take a moment to reflect on your biggest question or fear about death. Then, choose one way to move toward hope today:
  - Ask a mentor or trusted friend how they've found peace in God's promises about eternity.
  - Reach out to someone grieving—offer a listening ear, share a memory, or send them a message reminding them they're not alone.
  - Find a Bible passage about eternal life (like John 14:1–3 or Revelation 21:4), write it down, and reflect on how it speaks to your heart.

Prayer

God, loss feels overwhelming. The questions feel too big. Today, I bring You my grief, especially when I think about _____. Thank You for the hope You offer—that in You, separation is only temporary. Help me to trust Your promises and share that comfort with others who are hurting. Draw me closer to You, the only One who can hold eternity in His hands. Amen.

Deep Dive: Week 3 Review
Trusting His Perfect Timing

Timing can feel frustrating—especially when life doesn't unfold as expected. This week, we explored trusting God's timing instead of forcing our own. Solomon reminds us there is a time for everything under heaven.

God sees the bigger picture when we feel stuck. He stretches, refines, and teaches us in ways we may not yet understand. The key isn't just waiting—it's trusting that even slow seasons, unfair circumstances, and ordinary moments serve His purpose.

Pause and Reflect

1. What current "growing pain" might God be using to reshape you? How does this reframe your challenges?
2. View your relationships like a backpack—what strengthens you, and what weighs you down? What might God be calling you to release from this journey?
3. Where do you need God's perspective most—in change, ordinary routines, unfair situations, or loss? How does trusting His bigger plan shift your response?

Creative Expression

Express your journey of trust in one of these ways:

- Draw a plant with growth above ground and roots below—label both with what God is doing in your visible and invisible life.

- Create a "backpack inventory" of your relationships and experiences. What strengthens you? What weighs you down?

- Write a letter to yourself from God's perspective about a current challenge, contrasting His eternal view with your temporary one.

Truth to Remember

God is working in every moment—the visible and the invisible, the fair and the unfair, the ordinary and the eternal. Trust His process, even when you can't see the full picture yet.

Looking Ahead: Growing Through Authentic Connection

Trusting God's timing isn't meant to be a solo journey. He often uses friendships and mentors to guide us through seasons of waiting and uncertainty. **Week 4** will explore how the right relationships help us grow in faith, break free from comparison, and find encouragement along the way.

Get ready—this next week is about building real connections that help us grow.

WEEK 4

Growing Through Authentic Connection

Day 16
When Others Hurt

> *"Again I looked and saw all the oppression that was taking place under the sun: I saw the tears of the oppressed—and they have no comforter; power lies on the side of their oppressors—and they have no comforter."*
>
> **—Ecclesiastes 4:1**

You see them every day—the classmate who used to be talkative but now barely speaks, the coworker whose laughter never quite reaches their eyes, the friend who suddenly pulls away. Their pain is invisible beneath the casual *"I'm fine"* and rehearsed smiles that mask deeper wounds.

Solomon's words are haunting: *"They have no comforter."* Twice, he emphasizes this universal human need. Yet, how often do we look past signs of struggle, assume someone else will check in, or think we don't know what to say? Each missed opportunity deepens their isolation, confirming their fear that no one truly sees them.

Centuries later, Jesus stepped into this brokenness. He didn't avoid the wounded—He moved toward them. Quoting Isaiah, He declared: *"The Spirit of the Lord is on me … to set the oppressed free"* (Luke 4:18). He demonstrated this by touching those others avoided, sharing meals with the excluded, and stopping for those everyone ignored. Jesus noticed, stayed, and loved.

What if we did the same? Maybe comfort isn't about having all the right words—it's simply showing up. It's sitting beside someone who feels invisible, sending that "Hey, I'm thinking about you" text, or speaking up when someone is mocked. Being present, listening attentively, and responding compassionately matters far more than having all the answers.

Key Point

- This week, look intentionally for those who might be hurting. Challenge yourself to not just notice but also respond. Choose one action to take:
    - Save a seat for someone who usually sits alone.
    - Send a text checking in on a friend who's gone quiet.
    - If you notice something concerning, tell a trusted adult who can help.

- Think of a time when someone showed up for you in a difficult season. How did that impact you?

Prayer

> *Jesus, help me see the hidden hurts around me. When I feel the urge to look away, give me courage to step in. Show me how to be Your hands and feet—to notice, listen, and care. Help me trust You with their healing while being present in their pain. Amen.*

Day 17
Running Your Own Race

> *"And I saw that all toil and all achievement spring from one person's envy of another. This too is meaningless, a chasing after the wind."*
>
> **—Ecclesiastes 4:4**

You're scrolling through social media when you see it—someone just got into their dream school, landed the perfect internship, or announced the relationship you've been praying for. You're happy for them ... or at least you want to be. But deep down, it stings. *What about me? Why am I still waiting?*

Like a runner constantly glancing at other lanes, comparison throws us off balance. We see others crossing finish lines while our progress feels slow and uncertain. Each glance sideways makes us miss our own steps forward.

Comparison doesn't just steal our joy; it drains our confidence. Their success feels like a spotlight on our unfinished journey. We measure our struggles against their polished achievements, their confidence against our doubts, their straight path against our winding one. The more we compare, the deeper we spiral into insecurity.

But God never asked you to run someone else's race. He designed your journey uniquely—every twist and delay included. Paul reminds us: *"Each one should test their own actions. Then they can take pride in themselves alone, without comparing themselves to someone else"* (Galatians 6:4).

Maybe your path looks different— taking a gap year while friends head to college, choosing an unexpected major, or feeling stuck when everyone else seems to be moving forward. Different doesn't mean wrong. God is working in ways you can't see yet. Trust His timing, not theirs, and you'll stop chasing wind.

Key Point

God has a unique race for you—comparison only distracts you from running it well.

Live It Out

- Turn jealousy into inspiration by asking, "What does their success teach me about God's faithfulness?" rather than "Why them and not me?"

- Write down three ways you've grown this past year as a reminder that God is working in your story, even when the timing looks different.

- Celebrate someone whose success once made you jealous. Send them a genuine congratulatory message. Encouraging their journey actually strengthens yours.

Prayer

Father, teach me to trust Your perfect timing for my life. When I'm tempted to compare, remind me that You've called me to my own race, not theirs. Help me celebrate my growth, even when it looks different from others. Thank You for being faithful in every season. Amen.

Day 18
Breaking Free

"There was a man all alone ... There was no end to his toil, yet his eyes were not content ... 'For whom am I toiling,' he asked, 'and why am I depriving myself of enjoyment?'"

—**Ecclesiastes 4:8**

You sit in class, staring at the career path they say makes sense. You nod along to relationship advice that doesn't quite fit. You laugh at jokes that don't align with your values. Deep down, a voice whispers: *This isn't me.*

It's easy to get caught living for others' approval—pursuing a degree that sounds impressive, staying in a relationship because it looks good, following the worn path because stepping off feels risky. Like a bird taught to mimic others' melodies, your voice gets buried beneath expectations.

Solomon knew this feeling. He chased achievement, wealth, status—everything that was supposed to bring fulfillment—only to question it all. His words feel just as real today: *"For whom am I toiling, and why am I depriving myself of enjoyment?"*

But God never designed you to live as a copy of someone else. He formed you with a unique calling, whispering it to your heart before anyone else spoke over your life: *"Before I formed you in the womb I knew you, before you were born I set you apart"* (Jeremiah 1:5).

Your path might look different. Maybe you're called to pursue a passion others don't understand, or take a step that doesn't fit the usual script. Following your God-given path isn't defiance—it's obedience to a higher purpose.

Key Point
Your purpose isn't found in others' pressures, but in God's guidance.

Live It Out
- Take five minutes to answer these questions honestly:
    - If no one else's opinion mattered, what would I pursue?
    - Where in my life am I ignoring God's quiet direction because of others' expectations?
    - What's one small but bold step I can take this week to move toward my God-given purpose?
- Think of someone whose opinion weighs heavily on your decisions. What would it look like to release their expectations and trust God instead?

Prayer

> *Father, I'm tired of shaping my choices around others' expectations. Help me hear Your voice above the noise. Thank You for creating me with a unique purpose—not to mimic someone else's life, but to live the one You designed for me. Give me courage to take the next step. Amen.*

Day 19
Together We Stand

> *"Two are better than one, because they have a good return for their labor: If either of them falls down, one can help the other up ... Though one may be overpowered, two can defend themselves."*
>
> —Ecclesiastes 4:9–10,12

Marcus stared at the text message. Another elderly church member had missed a doctor's appointment because no one could take them. His heart sank. What could he do? He was just one person.

At first, the problem felt too big—too many people in need, not enough hands to help. But then he thought of his friends. *What if we all work together?*

A simple group chat turned into something more. Within weeks, a network of student volunteers had formed—giving rides, running errands, and checking in. What started as helplessness transformed into a movement of hope.

But the impact didn't stop there. Young volunteers found unexpected friendships with the seniors they helped. Their passengers, once feeling forgotten, discovered renewed joy in sharing their wisdom and experiences. Marcus had assumed this was just about meeting a need. Instead, God was creating a bridge between generations.

God designed us to walk alongside each other. True community isn't just about having people to hang out with—it's about strengthening each other, bearing burdens, and serving together. *"A friend loves at all times, and a brother is born for a time of adversity"* (Proverbs 17:17). Alone, we might struggle. But together, we become part of something greater.

Key Point
God strengthens us through a genuine community that serves together.

Live It Out
- Think about a time when someone's support made a difference in your life. Now ask:
    - Who around me needs that same kind of support?
    - Where is God calling me to step up and serve—not alone, but alongside others?
- This week, team up with friends to serve someone in need. Even something simple—offering a ride, helping with groceries, or checking in on someone feeling left out—can reveal God's love in practical ways.
- Think of one person struggling alone right now. Reach out today with a text, call, or invitation. Sometimes, just knowing someone cares makes all the difference.

Prayer

Lord, thank You for the strength found in community. Help me notice those who need support, and give me courage to step up with others. Show me how to use my gifts to serve those around me. Let our combined efforts reflect Your love. Amen.

Day 20
Unseen Wisdom

> *"Better a poor but wise youth than an old but foolish king who no longer knows how to heed a warning..."*
>
> —**Ecclesiastes 4:13**

You stand at a crossroads, uncertain. A decision looms, confusion swirls, and no clear direction emerges. Then, suddenly, wisdom appears—like finding a compass in the fog when you've lost your way. The needle points true regardless of who holds it.

This wisdom often comes from unexpected sources. Maybe it's a younger sibling casually stating something that hits deeper than they realize. Maybe it's a lyric from a song you've heard a hundred times, but today, it carries new meaning. Maybe it's a stranger's passing comment that lingers in your thoughts.

God's wisdom doesn't always arrive in obvious ways. The world measures wisdom by degrees, power, and status—prestigious titles and years of experience. But Solomon flips the script—a youth with an open heart can have more wisdom than a king who refuses to listen. True wisdom isn't found in seniority but in a teachable spirit.

Solomon reminds us: *"Listen to advice and accept discipline, and at the end you will be counted among the wise"* (Proverbs 19:20). This wisdom feels especially relevant in today's world of information overload, where discerning true insight requires a heart attuned to God's voice.

True wisdom isn't about how much you know. It's about how open you are to hearing what God is speaking—even when it comes from surprising places.

Key Point

God reveals His wisdom through unexpected sources if we are humble enough to listen.

Live It Out

- Think of a decision, problem, or question you've been struggling with. For the next three days, intentionally listen for unexpected wisdom:
  - Pay attention to the quiet people around you. What do they see that others miss?
  - Ask someone younger than you for their perspective. You might be surprised.
  - Pray for discernment, then look for wisdom in unexpected places—conversations, books, songs, Scripture.
- Write down any surprising insight you receive. At the end of three days, reflect on how God might be speaking through these sources.

Prayer

Lord, give me a heart that listens. Help me recognize Your wisdom, even when it comes from places I don't expect. Teach me to stay humble, open, and teachable—never too proud to hear the truth You are speaking. Thank You for the ways You guide me, even when I don't realize it in the moment. Amen.

Deep Dive: Week 4 Review
Strength in Authentic Community

Life was never meant to be lived alone. We were created for connection, designed to support one another through relationships that reflect God's love. This week, we explored how God strengthens us through authentic friendships, shared purpose, and unexpected voices.

Deep relationships require intentionality, vulnerability, and courage. It's easy to let comparison, expectations, or past hurts keep us distant. Yet, when we embrace God's design for community, our greatest growth often happens alongside others.

Solomon reminds us that two are better than one—when one falls, the other can help them up. Authentic relationships aren't just about having people around; they're about walking through life together.

Pause and Reflect

1. Where did you notice hidden pain this week? How might God be inviting you to be present for someone struggling?

2. In what areas have you been comparing yourself to others? What would it mean to run your own race, focused on God's unique path for you?

3. When have you encountered God's wisdom through an unexpected source? How did it shape your understanding?

Creative Expression

Choose a way to explore what you've learned about authentic connection:

- Write a note of encouragement to someone who might be hurting.

- Journal about a moment when choosing your authentic path required courage.

- Create a simple plan for how you and two to three friends could serve together this month.

Truth to Remember

God speaks through authentic community and unexpected voices, guiding us to serve together while embracing our unique paths.

Looking Ahead: Moving Past the Surface

This week, we saw how deep relationships require intentionality, honesty, and courage. But deep relationships don't just connect us with others—they prepare us for a deeper walk with God. **Week 5** will challenge us to move beyond shallow faith, routine prayers, and passive belief to truly know God—not just know about Him.

Get ready—this next week is about pursuing a faith that is real, personal, and deeply rooted.

WEEK 5

Moving Past the Surface

Day 21
Breaking Through the Noise

"Guard your steps when you go to the house of God. Go near to listen rather than to offer the sacrifice of fools, who do not know that they do wrong."

—Ecclesiastes 5:1

The second you wake up, noise greets you. Your phone lights up. Your playlist hums in the background. Conversations and notifications pull your focus in every direction. Even when you're alone, your mind is busy—replaying past conversations, planning the next task, filling every gap with content and scrolling.

In this constant motion, when do you truly hear God?

Our generation drowns in noise. Prayer competes with messages. Worship fights against endless distractions. Even when we sit with God, our minds race to the next thing. Like a radio caught between stations, we struggle to focus on His voice in the static.

Yet God still calls us to listen. Just as He spoke to Elijah, not through wind, earthquake, or fire, but in a gentle whisper (1 Kings 19:11–12), He speaks today—not through chaos, but in stillness. *"Be still, and know that I am God"* (Psalm 46:10).

This is more than just silence. It's quieting our hearts. We often rush to God with lists of requests but never pause to hear His response.

But when we slow down—truly slow down—His peace silences distractions. His love becomes clearer. His truth anchors our wandering minds.

God isn't competing for your attention. He's waiting for you to make space.

Key Point

When we quiet our hearts, God's whisper rises above the noise.

Live It Out

- Take three intentional steps today:
  - Recognize the noise: Note your top three distractions from God.
  - Create stillness: Find ten minutes in silence before God—no distractions. If your mind wanders, gently return to Him.
  - Replace the noise: Instead of filling every gap with content, choose Scripture, prayer, or worship. Notice how it changes your day.
- For one hour today, fast from noise. No media or entertainment. Be fully present. What do you notice? What does God say when you make space to listen?

Prayer

Lord, in this noisy world, teach me to listen. Help me recognize distractions. Make Your voice louder than my worries, clearer than distractions. Quiet my heart so I can hear what You've been saying all along. Amen.

Day 22
Vending Machine Prayers

"Do not be quick with your mouth, do not be hasty in your heart to utter anything before God. God is in heaven and you are on earth, so let your words be few."

—Ecclesiastes 5:2

You stand before a vending machine, dollar in hand. Press the right buttons, and you get your snack. But sometimes, nothing happens—the machine jams, your snack gets stuck, or worse, it just eats your money. No refund, no explanation.

Prayer can feel like that. "If You help me pass this test, I'll read my Bible more." "If You make them like me, I'll never miss church." Each desperate deal tries to unlock the right combination of words to get what you need. But what happens when God doesn't "deliver"?

Bargaining prayers often come from fear, not faith—the panic of seeing a test you're not ready for, the helplessness of watching your parents fight, the ache of rejection. When God seems silent, the deal-making escalates. We don't just want answers; we want control.

But God isn't a vending machine. He's a Father. When Jesus taught prayer, He didn't begin with demands or negotiations. Instead, He said, *"Our Father..."* (Matthew 6:9). True prayer starts not with requests, but with relationship.

God isn't looking for perfectly phrased bargains—He wants honest hearts willing to trust Him, even when the answer doesn't come right away. The Creator already knows what you need. The real question is: Are you willing to wait and trust Him?

Key Point

God wants a real relationship, not a business deal.

Live It Out

- Look back at your recent prayers. Do any sound like "if-then" bargains? Rewrite them as trust-based prayers:
  - Instead of "If You help me on this test, I'll read my Bible," try, "God, help me work hard and trust You, even if the outcome isn't perfect."
  - Instead of "If You fix this friendship, I'll never complain," pray, "God, teach me to handle relationships with wisdom, whether restored or not."
- Choose one important prayer request. Express your need, but deliberately leave the solution part unfinished—no suggestions or conditions. Simply trust God with the outcome.
- Think of a time when God answered differently than expected—but better. Share your story with a friend.

Prayer

Father, forgive my need to bargain. Help me trust, even when You seem silent. Thank You that I am Your child—not Your customer. Transform my deals into dialogue, my panic into patience. Amen.

Day 23
Worth the Work

"The sleep of a laborer is sweet, whether they eat little or much, but as for the rich, their abundance permits them no sleep ... wealth hoarded to the harm of its owners."

—**Ecclesiastes 5:12–13**

Like a climber reaching a hard-earned summit, there's something profoundly rewarding about achieving goals through mental or physical effort. Your body aches, your eyes feel heavy, but the satisfaction of finishing a hard day's work runs deep. Whether it's finally buying your own used car after months of early shifts, seeing your grades improve after late-night study sessions, or saving enough for a short-term mission trip, the reward isn't just in the result—it's in knowing you did this.

But we live in a world that wants everything now. Streaming eliminates waiting. Same-day shipping makes buying effortless. Social media showcases success without showing the struggle. The problem? Quick gains often leave us feeling empty. When success comes without effort, it lacks meaning.

God designed work not as punishment, but as a gift. *"In all labor there is profit, but mere talk leads only to poverty"* (Proverbs 14:23). More than just a paycheck, hard work teaches resilience, responsibility, and confidence. It builds more than wealth—it builds you.

Key Point

The satisfaction of earned success runs deeper than anything simply given.

Live It Out

- Think about something you've worked hard for—a job, a sport, a personal project, or even overcoming a struggle:
  - What did you sacrifice to achieve it?
  - What did you gain beyond the reward itself? (Patience, discipline, problem-solving?)
  - How can you apply that same work ethic to your current goals?

- Choose one small task today that you've been putting off. Complete it with excellence, then take a moment to notice how it feels to finish something well.

Prayer

Lord, help me value earned rewards over easy gains. Give me patience when the process feels slow and wisdom to pursue work that strengthens both my skills and my character. Thank You for the satisfaction that comes through effort and for shaping me through the journey. Amen.

Day 24
Finding Joy in the Journey

> *"Then I realized that it is good and proper for a person to eat and drink, and to find satisfaction in their work ... When God gives someone wealth and possessions, and the ability to enjoy them, to accept their lot and be happy in their work—this is a gift of God."*
>
> **—Ecclesiastes 5:18–19**

It's easy to feel like real life is always just ahead. Maybe you're stuck in a boring class, working a job that barely pays for gas, or waiting for the moment when your dreams finally start coming true. Everything right now feels like a stepping stone to something better. You tell yourself, "Once I graduate ... once I land that job ... once I reach that goal—then I'll be happy." But what if God wants to give you joy right now, in this season?

Paul offers a different perspective: *"Whatever you do, work at it with all your heart, as working for the Lord"* (Colossians 3:23). Contentment isn't about finally arriving at success—it's about embracing the journey itself. It doesn't mean giving up on your dreams but realizing God is already moving in your life today.

That class you can't stand? It's sharpening your patience. The job you don't love? It's teaching you responsibility. The delays and detours? They're shaping your character. When we start seeing even the most ordinary tasks as part of God's work in us, frustration turns into purpose.

Key Point

Contentment isn't about having everything you want, but learning to want what God has already given you.

Live It Out

- Think about one task you dislike right now—homework, chores, or your part-time job. Instead of just enduring it, ask:
  - How might God be using this to teach me something?
  - What's one way I can approach it with joy?
  - How can I make this moment an act of worship, then tackle that task with a fresh perspective this week?

- Reflect on a time you were impatient for the next step but later saw God's purpose in that season. Share your story with someone—your experience might help them appreciate their own journey.

Prayer

Father, help me find joy not in future success alone, but in today's work. Open my eyes to Your presence in my daily routine. Teach me contentment where I am while still striving to grow. Thank You for the gift of meaningful work and the satisfaction it brings. Amen.

Day 25
Reality Check

"What the eye sees is better than what the soul desires. This too is meaningless, a chasing after the wind."

—Ecclesiastes 6:9

You're scrolling through social media, seeing one perfect highlight after another. Someone landed their dream internship. Another is on vacation. Someone else posts their perfect relationship. Meanwhile, your reality feels ... ordinary.

It's easy to romanticize a version of life that always seems just out of reach. Like a funhouse mirror that stretches and warps what we see, our minds paint elaborate pictures of how life "should" be. We dream about the ideal relationship, the dream career, the perfect version of ourselves. We believe that happiness is waiting just beyond our current circumstances.

But what happens when reality doesn't measure up to those dreams? Discontent creeps in. The real moments of life feel dull compared to the expectations we've created. We start chasing fantasies instead of building something real.

Ecclesiastes challenges this mindset. Dreams without action are just illusions. Jesus reinforces this when He tells us: *"Therefore do not worry about tomorrow, for tomorrow will worry about itself"* (Matthew 6:34). God calls us to be fully present in the life He's given us today.

Your dreams are not bad. They are meant to guide you forward, not keep you stuck in dissatisfaction. When we focus too much on what could be, we miss what God is doing right now—transforming both you and your dreams along the way.

Key Point

God gives us dreams to inspire action, not to escape the present.

Live It Out

- Pause for a moment. Look around at your current reality. What's one aspect of your life that you've been overlooking or taking for granted because you're too focused on what's next?

- Write down three things you appreciate about where you are right now.

- Now, take one small, real step toward a future goal. It could be sending an email, researching a skill, or finishing something you've been avoiding.

Prayer

> *Father, thank You for the dreams You place in my heart. Help me recognize the difference between hopeful vision and unhealthy escape. Teach me to be present in what You're doing today while trusting You with the future. Let me take action toward my goals, without missing Your presence in my current reality. Amen.*

Deep Dive: Week 5 Review
Finding Joy in What's Real

In a world of distractions and quick-fix solutions, real faith requires intentionality. This past week, we explored creating space for God's voice, engaging in meaningful prayer, and choosing action over fantasy.

Solomon reminds us in Ecclesiastes 2:24 that joy isn't found in chasing perfection or temporary highs—it's found in meeting God in real, messy, and ordinary moments. Often, it's not the obvious distractions but the small, constant interruptions that pull us from an authentic connection with God, who meets us in our struggles, waiting, and ordinary routines.

Pause and Reflect

1. Which distractions most often compete with your time with God? What practical steps from Day 21 have helped you create more space for listening?

2. How has your prayer life changed since exploring the difference between bargaining and relationship with God? What's one way you've experienced God as a Father rather than a "vending machine"?

3. Where do you see yourself most tempted to escape into fantasy rather than engage with reality? How might God be inviting you to take action in that area?

Creative Expression

Choose one way to deepen your faith and apply what you've learned:

- Design your "quiet zone" for prayer and document how it impacts your time with God.

- Write a letter to God expressing your heart without any bargaining or deals.

- Take one practical step toward a dream you've been fantasizing about.

Truth to Remember

God meets us in the real moments—the quiet, the struggle, the ordinary routines. He's not waiting for perfect circumstances or polished prayers but invites us into authentic relationship right where we are.

Looking Ahead: When Faith Gets Tested

Pursuing real faith is one thing—holding onto it when life gets hard is another. **Week 6** will challenge us to stand firm when circumstances shake us, and God's plan feels unclear. How do we respond when things don't match our expectations or when we don't see the answers right away?

Get ready—this next week is about developing a faith that lasts through every season.

WEEK 6

When Faith Gets Tested

Day 26
When Life Hits Hard

"... and the day of death better than the day of birth ... The heart of the wise is in the house of mourning."

—Ecclesiastes 7:1,4

One moment, everything is normal. Then suddenly, it isn't. A text message. A phone call. A conversation you never expected to have. Loss crashes into your world, and suddenly, nothing feels the same.

Pain changes you. Like a broken bone that heals stronger at the fracture point, your deepest growth often comes through your deepest struggles. The end of a friendship. A shattered dream. Watching someone you love suffer. These moments feel unfair, unbearable—and yet, they shape you in ways that easy times never could.

It feels harsh—even strange—to think that wisdom is found in mourning rather than in celebration. But loss strips away illusions of control. It forces you to face questions that comfort never demands. The reality of grief shifts your perspective past the temporary, forcing you to wrestle with what truly lasts.

Centuries after Solomon, Jesus affirmed this truth: *"Blessed are those who mourn, for they will be comforted"* (Matthew 5:4). He doesn't tell us to seek suffering, but He does promise that in it, we will meet

Him in ways joy alone could never reveal. He doesn't just remove pain; He transforms us through it.

Key Point

Loss clears your vision—suddenly, you see what truly matters.

Live It Out

- Think about how loss has shifted your perspective:
    - If you're grieving, write down one truth your pain is revealing about faith, love, or what truly matters. When you're ready, share it with a trusted friend.
    - If you're supporting someone who's hurting, be the friend who saves a seat, sends a text, and stays when others drift away.
- Think of someone who has walked through grief with faith and resilience. Ask them what helped them find peace in the middle of loss. Their perspective might give you a glimpse of the wisdom God is forming in your own life.

Prayer

God, when loss feels too heavy to carry, help me see beyond the pain to the wisdom You're building in me. Give me the courage to face hard truths instead of hiding in distractions. Show me how to honor memories by living with purpose and authentic love. Help me be there for others who are hurting, too. Comfort us as only You can. Amen.

Day 27
Beyond Performance

"Do not be over-righteous, neither be over-wise—why destroy yourself?"

—**Ecclesiastes 7:16**

Faith can start to feel like an impossible balancing act. You try not to seem too religious around non-believing friends, but also don't want to disappoint your church circle. You're navigating skeptical comments from classmates, expectations from youth group, and your own inner voice whispering, "Are you even doing this right?"

Like a tightrope walker terrified of falling, you carefully adjust every step—afraid that one wrong move might send your spiritual life crashing. You try harder. You read more. You pray longer. Yet, instead of feeling closer to God, it feels like you're just getting better at performing.

But Solomon exposes something we don't often talk about: Trying to "look" like the perfect Christian can be its own kind of struggle. Paul reminds us: *"My grace is sufficient for you, for my power is made perfect in weakness"* (2 Corinthians 12:9). God never asked for a flawless routine—He wants an *honest* relationship.

When you wrestle with faith questions, when you feel distant from God, when worship doesn't stir your emotions—these aren't failures. They're moments of honest seeking. Real faith isn't about appearing righteous; it's about staying real with God. He doesn't base His love on how "worthy" you seem. He invites you to bring your doubts and struggles, not to stay stuck, but to grow deeper together.

Key Point

Real faith isn't a performance—it thrives in authenticity.

Live It Out

- Take a moment to be completely real with God. Write down one area where you feel pressure to be the "perfect Christian." Then, instead of hiding it, talk to God about it in prayer.

- If you're comfortable, share it with a mentor, small group leader, or friend who loves both God and you. Ask them how they learned to stop performing and start being authentic.

- Consider someone in your life who might be struggling with perfectionism in their faith journey. Reach out and remind them that following Jesus isn't about appearing flawless—it's about genuine relationship with Him.

Prayer

Father, I've been trying so hard to measure up. But You're not asking me to perform—You're asking me to be honest. Help me take off the mask. Thank You that Your grace meets me in every doubt, every struggle, every moment of searching. Teach me to walk with You, no pretending—just real faith. Amen.

Day 28
When Heroes Fall

"Indeed, there is no one on earth who is righteous, no one who does what is right and never sins."

—Ecclesiastes 7:20

The moment you hear the news, it feels like the ground shifts beneath you. That mentor you trusted, the leader who shaped your faith, the voice you believed was steady and unshakable—suddenly, they're not who you thought they were. The disappointment is sharp, and you wonder: *If they couldn't get it right, how can I trust anything anymore?*

It's painful when someone you admire reveals their humanity in the worst way. Maybe it's a pastor caught in scandal, a mentor who let you down, or a leader whose life didn't match their message. Their fall doesn't just break trust—it cracks something deeper. *If they were wrong, was I wrong to believe them? If they failed, is my faith failing, too?*

We elevate leaders, forgetting they're human just like us—then feel betrayed when they prove it. The psalmist understood this human tendency when he warned, *"Do not put your trust in princes, in human beings, who cannot save"* (Psalm 146:3). No leader, no matter how gifted, was ever meant to be your foundation. Their faithfulness may waver, but God's never will.

Your hope isn't in perfect role models—it's in a perfect God. People fail, but Jesus never does. Leaders may stumble, but grace remains steady, covering not just their failures but ours, too. When human pedestals crumble, God's love stands unshaken.

Key Point

People will fail us—God's faithfulness never will.

Live It Out

- Think of one leader or mentor you admire. Ask yourself:
  - Have I put them on a pedestal?
  - Am I building my faith on Christ or on the people who teach me about Him?

- Take a moment to pray for them—not as someone who has it all together, but as someone who needs grace just like you do.

- Have you ever struggled with trusting God after a leader disappointed you? Talk with a mentor or friend about how to process spiritual disillusionment without losing faith.

Prayer

Father, it's hard when those I look up to fall short. Help me remember that no human is perfect, and no leader is meant to be my foundation. When disappointment shakes me, anchor me in Your unshakable faithfulness. Teach me to respect people, but to worship only You. Amen.

Day 29
When Answers Aren't Enough

> *"All this I tested by wisdom ... but this was beyond me. Whatever exists is far off and most profound—who can discover it?"*
>
> —**Ecclesiastes 7:23–24**

It happens in a moment—the belief you never questioned suddenly doesn't make sense. Maybe it's a Bible passage that feels at odds with science, or a prayer that goes unanswered. Maybe it's watching good people suffer while the dishonest thrive. Suddenly, your faith, once so steady, feels like a thread unraveling in your hands.

Doubt doesn't always arrive loudly. Sometimes, it's a slow, creeping uncertainty, whispering, What if you've been wrong all along? One day, you feel sure of what you believe. The next, the foundation feels shaky. Faith on Sunday can feel unshakable, but by Wednesday, it's under siege.

You're not alone in this tension. Solomon, with all his wisdom, admitted there were things he couldn't comprehend. Even Job, Thomas, and John the Baptist—people of incredible faith—struggled with deep questions. Their doubts didn't push them away from God; they became pathways to deeper understanding.

Maybe faith was never meant to be about having every answer. Paul reminds us: *"Now I know in part; then I shall know fully"* (1

Corinthians 13:12). Faith isn't the absence of doubt—it's choosing to trust God in the unknown. Your questions don't make you weak; they mean you're seeking something real. And that search? It doesn't lead away from God—it leads deeper into Him.

Key Point

Questions don't weaken faith—they give it room to grow.

Live It Out

- Write down the hardest faith question on your heart right now. Then:
  - Pray about it honestly, without holding back.
  - Find someone who will walk with you in the wondering without rushing to explain it away.
  - Look up one biblical figure who wrestled with doubt and see how God met them in it.

- Have you ever had a question or doubt that actually strengthened your faith rather than weakened it? Share your experience—your story might encourage someone else who's wrestling with difficult questions.

Prayer

> *God, when science and Scripture seem to clash, when suffering doesn't make sense, when my prayers feel like they're hitting a wall—thank You that You don't turn away from my questions. Help me bring my doubts to You instead of burying them. Teach me to trust You, not just in what I understand, but in what I don't. Amen.*

Day 30
The Sweet Trap

"I find more bitter than death the woman who is a snare, whose heart is a trap and whose hands are chains..."

—Ecclesiastes 7:26

Temptation rarely looks dangerous at first. It weaves its web slowly, strand by strand, waiting for the right moment to tighten. A harmless joke becomes flirtation. A private message turns into a secret. A small compromise, just once—then once more.

The trap isn't sprung all at once; it's set with precision—a well-placed compliment, the thrill of being pursued, the whispered promise of something just for you. "No one will know." "It's not a big deal." "Your friends wouldn't understand." The rush of feeling wanted clashes with a quiet pang of unease. But by the time the tension turns to regret, the chains have already tightened.

Solomon warns, *"Keep to a path far from her; do not go near the door of her house"* (Proverbs 5:8). The time to resist isn't when the web is wrapped around you—it's before you step into it. Real relationships don't rely on secrecy; they flourish in the light. Anything that requires hiding, lying, or compromising your values isn't love—it's a trap.

Key Point

The sweetest bait often hides the sharpest hook.

Live It Out

- Think about a relationship or situation that feels exciting but uneasy. Ask yourself:
    - Would I feel comfortable if others knew about this?
    - Is this pulling me closer to God or further from Him?
    - If a friend told me they were in this situation, what advice would I give them?

- Take action:
    - Talk to a trusted friend or mentor.
    - Block or distance yourself from contacts leading you toward compromise.
    - Decide today to choose character over regret.

- Temptation extends beyond relationships to anything drawing us away from God—dishonesty, addiction, gossip, or self-destructive thoughts. Read 1 Corinthians 10:13 and consider your personal "way out" when temptation approaches. Memorize this verse and place it somewhere visible daily.

Prayer

Father, help me see past sweet words to true intentions. Give me the strength to walk away from temptation before it traps me. Thank You for real love strengthening faith, not weakening it. Help me be a person of character, choosing You over compromise. Amen.

Deep Dive: Week 6 Review
Finding Hope in Hard Places

Faith feels easy when everything's going well. But what about when life hits hard—when relationships break, plans fail, or questions go unanswered?

Solomon reminds us that faith isn't about avoiding difficulties; it's about having someone walk through them with you. Whether you're dealing with loss, disappointment, waiting, or mistakes, you don't have to face it alone.

Pause and Reflect

1. Which of this week's devotionals touched the most tender part of your spiritual journey—your grief, your challenges with performance, your disappointment in leaders, your unanswered questions, or your battles with temptation?

2. Where do you feel most vulnerable in your faith right now? What makes that particular struggle especially challenging?

3. How has bringing your authentic self to God—with all your doubts and questions—changed your understanding of His love?

Creative Expression

Choose one way to process what you've learned and how God is strengthening you through difficult seasons:

- Write an honest prayer about your current situation.

- Create a playlist that captures your journey with God—both the questions and the trust.

- Draw or describe your faith journey as a path, marking both the valleys and mountaintops.

Truth to Remember

God meets you in the profound moments of adversity—whether in grief, doubt, disappointment, or temptation. His love remains steady when everything else feels uncertain.

Looking Ahead: Wisdom for Life's Challenges

This week, we wrestled with the hard questions of faith. But sometimes, the wisdom we need isn't just about understanding struggles—it's about knowing how to navigate life with a godly perspective. **Week 7** will help us explore how to apply biblical wisdom to real-life situations—relationships, decisions, disappointments, and the search for purpose. Solomon spent his life pursuing wisdom, and his words still hold practical, life-giving truths for us today.

Get ready—this next week is about discovering the wisdom that shapes how we live every day.

WEEK 7

Wisdom for Life's Challenges

Day 31
Facing Authority

"Obey the king's command, I say, because you took an oath before God."

—Ecclesiastes 8:2

The moment happens without warning. Maybe it's your coach benching you despite your dedication. Your teacher is mocking your faith in front of the class. A boss unfairly shifts blame onto you. Like being caught in a sudden storm, these moments shake your confidence, making you question whether speaking up is worth the risk—or if staying silent means surrendering your integrity.

Dealing with difficult authority isn't just frustrating—it feels personal. It tests your patience, character, and faith. The urge to lash out or retreat into resentment is strong. But both reactions leave scars—either on your relationships or within your heart.

So what now? Submission doesn't mean surrendering who you are. *"Submit to one another out of reverence for Christ"* (Ephesians 5:21). True submission is strength under control. When a decision feels unfair, responding with maturity opens the door to real influence. Try:

- When facing unrealistic demands: "I want to excel. Could we explore approaches that help me deliver my best work?"

- When your faith is challenged: Let your actions reflect your beliefs louder than words.

- When instructions backfire: "Help me understand where this went wrong and how I can improve."

These responses step into the moment with both humility and courage. Your ability to navigate with grace prepares you for every leadership role in your future.

Key Point

True strength emerges in how you handle authority, especially when you disagree.

Live It Out

- Before confronting an unfair decision, ask yourself:
    - What happened? Define the issue clearly.
    - Why does it feel unfair? Identify if it's personal frustration or a genuine injustice.
    - What change do I seek? Approach with a goal, not just a complaint.

- Present your concerns respectfully, with willingness to work together. The greatest influence comes from wisdom and grace, not rebellion.

- Think about a time when you handled an authority conflict well—or when you wish you had done it differently. What did you learn?

Prayer

> *Lord, when authority feels unfair, help me pause before reacting. Grant me wisdom to voice concerns with respect, courage to stand firm with dignity, and discernment to know when to speak or step back. Show me how to build bridges that reflect Your character. Amen.*

Day 32
When Control Slips Away

> *"No one has power over the wind to contain it; so no one has power over the time of their death."*
>
> —**Ecclesiastes 8:8**

It happens in an instant—the moment control vanishes from your grasp. The text goes unread. The phone call never comes. The medical update offers more uncertainty than clarity. Like a swimmer caught in a riptide, you fight for control, gasping for certainty, desperate to stop life from slipping further out of reach.

Kaitlyn grips her phone, her pulse pounding with each unanswered message. Ever since her brother's accident, every delay sends her spiraling. *What if the doctors are wrong? What if something happens while she's not there? What if her world never feels safe again?* She used to believe that if she planned enough, prayed enough, stayed alert enough, she could keep everything together. But now, that illusion is unraveling.

Anxiety thrives in the gap between what we wish we could control and what's actually in our hands. Some respond by obsessing over details, tracking every move. Others collapse beneath the weight, frozen by fear. But there's another way.

"Cast all your anxiety on him because he cares for you" (1 Peter 5:7). Kaitlyn still worries about her brother, but something shifts when she prays—not a magic fix, but a quiet presence meeting her panic with peace. As she releases her grip on control, she discovers a deeper strength. One that doesn't come from holding on but from letting go.

Key Point

Peace comes not from controlling life, but from yielding to God when there's nothing you can do.

Live It Out

- Write down two lists: One with what's in your control and another with what isn't. While you can't control outcomes, you can take small actions—praying, encouraging someone, choosing rest.

- Physically open your hands and pray: "Father, I trust You with what I can't do." Make this a habit when control feels impossible.

- Reach out to someone who's struggling: Remind them they don't have to carry everything alone. Have you ever had a moment where you surrendered something to God and felt peace in return? Share your story—your experience might be what someone needs to hear today.

Prayer

Father, my heart aches when I can't fix things or control what happens next. Teach me to recognize when it's time to stop striving and simply rest in You. Thank You that even when I reach the end of my strength, You remain steady. Amen.

Day 33
Into the Unknown

"No one knows what is coming—who can tell someone else what will happen after them?"

—Ecclesiastes 9:1

The email subject line blinks at you: *Industry Shift: The Rise of AI in Tech.* You hesitate before opening it, already dreading what you'll read. Another article predicting job losses. Another wave of uncertainty. The coding bootcamp you were so excited about last month? Now, it feels like a sinking ship. Maybe this career isn't as secure as you thought. Maybe all the time, effort, and tuition will lead to nothing. The unknown stretches before you, thick as fog on an unmarked trail.

Uncertainty breeds fear, but it also creates space for something else: possibility. While some jobs fade, new opportunities arise. Skills you're gaining now—problem-solving, adaptability, creative thinking—might prove more valuable than the specific path you initially planned. What feels like a dead end today could be the unexpected turn that leads somewhere better.

"In their hearts humans plan their course, but the Lord establishes their steps" (Proverbs 16:9). Planning isn't pointless—it's wise. Research, prepare, and make the best decisions you can. But expecting certainty? That's not yours to hold. The real challenge isn't just

choosing a path—it's learning to walk forward, even when you can't see every step ahead.

Key Point

You don't have to see the whole trail to trust the One guiding you.

Live It Out

- Write down your biggest fear about the future. Then, next to it, list:
  - One practical step you can take today.
  - One truth about God's character that anchors you in uncertainty.

- Share your list with a mentor who can pray with you and offer wisdom from their own journey.

- Do one small act of courage today—apply for that opportunity, send the email, take the first step forward, even if the whole path isn't clear yet. Have you ever stepped into the unknown and later realized God was guiding you all along? Share your story—it might be the encouragement someone else needs.

Prayer

> *Father, the unknown makes me anxious. I want guarantees, but You call me to trust. Help me plan wisely while relying completely on You. When fear whispers that I might fail, remind me that You establish my steps. Thank You that I don't have to walk this journey alone. Amen.*

Day 34
Love Worth Waiting For

> *"Enjoy life with your wife, whom you love, all the days of this meaningless life that God has given you under the sun."*
>
> **—Ecclesiastes 9:9**

You sit across from your friend as she talks about her new relationship. It all happened fast—dates turned into sleepovers, and now they're practically living together. Amanda laughs, calling it "just convenient," but you notice the hesitation in her voice. The excitement is already laced with uncertainty. You've seen this before—people diving into romance without a foundation, hoping passion will fill the gaps that patience was meant to build.

Love, when rushed, is like trying to satisfy hunger with pictures of food. It looks fulfilling but leaves you empty. Swipe right, hook up, settle for less—culture's shortcuts promise excitement but rarely deliver lasting connection. Lust offers passion without commitment, pleasure without security. But the thrill fades, and hearts often end up more wounded than fulfilled.

"Do not arouse or awaken love until it so desires" (Song of Solomon 2:7). This verse isn't about denying love—it's about protecting its timing. Culture treats boundaries as obstacles, but they're safeguards. Amanda's story is familiar: Relationships built on conve-

nience instead of commitment lead to quiet fears about where things are going. Real intimacy isn't rushed—it's cultivated.

But God's design offers more. Marriage is where love deepens, trust grows, and two people experience something real. It's not about waiting passively; it's about preparing intentionally. This season of singleness is a gift—an opportunity to develop financial wisdom, emotional maturity, spiritual depth, and self-discipline. **These aren't just life skills; they're marriage essentials.**

Key Point
Love built on God's timing isn't just worth waiting for—it's worth *preparing* for.

Live It Out

- List five qualities you desire in a future spouse. Then ask yourself: "Am I actively developing these same qualities in my own life?"

- Identify one way you can guard your heart this month—whether by setting boundaries, prioritizing friendships, or deepening your faith before seeking commitment.

- Start preparing now. Instead of focusing on finding the "right person," focus on becoming the person God has called you to be.

Prayer

Lord, help me honor love as You designed it—not as culture distorts it. Give me wisdom to wait when needed, strength to protect my heart, and patience to prepare for a love that reflects Your purpose. Thank You that real love isn't built in haste but in faithfulness. Amen.

Day 35
Small Choices, Big Impact

> *"Dead flies give perfume a bad smell; a little folly outweighs wisdom and honor."*
>
> —**Ecclesiastes 10:1**

A careless joke, a sarcastic comment, a private message screenshotted and shared—one tap, send, regret. What started as a small moment spirals into something devastating—a friendship shattered, a reputation tainted. In today's digital world, your smallest mistake can spread like a virus racing through social media, impossible to contain once released. The damage isn't theoretical—it's real, immediate, and continues to replicate long after.

Whether spreading gossip, venting online, or reacting in anger, these minor choices can contaminate what you've worked so hard to create. What feels insignificant now can transform into a viral moment that follows you for years.

"Let your speech always be gracious, seasoned with salt" (Colossians 4:6, ESV). This wisdom isn't just about your words—it's about preventing your character from becoming infected. The harder choice is usually the right one. Pausing before speaking, stepping away before reacting, choosing integrity over impulse—these decisions might cost you temporary validation, but they protect something

more valuable: a reputation that remains uncompromised when tested.

This truth extends beyond screens. Choosing what's right when no one's watching, remaining silent when gossip flows, maintaining integrity when deception feels easier—these small, consistent choices keep your character from contamination. Every time you choose honor over convenience, you're not just avoiding the virus of compromise; you're strengthening your immunity against future temptations.

Key Point

Protect your character—it's infinitely easier to maintain than repair.

Live It Out

- Before you post, text, or speak today, PAUSE:
    - Purpose: What am I trying to achieve?
    - Affect: Who could this impact?
    - Uplift: Does this build or destroy?
    - Seek: Is this wise?
    - Eternal: Does this reflect who I want to be?
- Let today's choices reflect who you're becoming.
- Think back to the last text or post you or a friend regretted sending. What could have changed the outcome? Share one insight from today's reflection—your experience might help someone else navigate the weight of small decisions.

Prayer

Lord, guard my words and actions with Your wisdom. When impulse tempts me, help me pause and reflect. Protect the purity of my character in these small moments so that my life isn't defined by viral mistakes but by consistent integrity. Make me someone whose influence draws others to You. Amen.

Deep Dive: Week 7 Review
Choosing Wisdom in Daily Life

Every day, we make choices that shape who we're becoming. This past week, we explored walking in wisdom—how we respond to authority, handle uncertainty, surrender control, pursue relationships, and make decisions that impact our future.

Solomon reminds us in Ecclesiastes 8:1 that wisdom isn't just knowledge—it's action. It's choosing faith over fear, integrity over shortcuts, and surrender over control. True wisdom starts with seeking God first, even when the next step isn't clear.

Pause and Reflect

1. Which challenge feels most pressing in your life right now—responding to difficult authority, releasing control, navigating uncertainty, resisting relationship shortcuts, or guarding your digital choices?

2. Looking back at this week, what decision seemed small but carried a greater impact than you expected?

3. How does knowing God guides each step change your approach to these challenges?

Creative Expression

Choose one way to explore what you've learned about wisdom in daily life:

- Journal: Write about a specific choice you made this week and how wisdom influenced that decision.

- Create a "Decision Map" showing three small decisions and their potential five-year impact.

- Write two endings to a recent challenge—one choosing wisdom and one choosing impulse.

Truth to Remember

Your daily choices are building tomorrow's character, one wise decision at a time.

Looking Ahead: Living for What Lasts

Wisdom helps us navigate life's daily choices, but what about the bigger picture? What happens when we shift our focus from temporary things to what truly lasts? **Week 8** will challenge us to evaluate what we're investing our time, energy, and hearts into. Are we chasing things that fade away, or are we building a legacy that carries eternal value?

Get ready—this next week is about choosing what lasts beyond this life.

WEEK 8

Living for What Lasts

Day 36
The Unexpected Power of Giving

> *"Cast your bread upon the waters, for after many days you will find it again. Give portions to seven, yes to eight, for you do not know what disaster may come upon the land."*
>
> —Ecclesiastes 11:1–2

You're down to your last few dollars for the week, and a friend forgets their lunch. Do you share or hold on to what little you have? At Bible study, you slip what's left of your cash into a collection for trafficking survivors, feeling both conviction and hesitation. Generosity sounds noble when there's abundance—but when you're barely getting by, giving can feel reckless.

In ancient Egypt, farmers would cast seed onto flooded fields, trusting it would sink into fertile soil and later yield a harvest. On the surface, throwing seed into water seems wasteful, even foolish. Yet, Solomon uses this image to teach us about trust. Like a boomerang thrown into the air, what we give might seem lost at first. But just as the boomerang returns, our giving comes back, often in unexpected ways.

"Give, and it will be given to you. A good measure, pressed down, shaken together and running over, will be poured into your lap" (Luke 6:38). That lunch money you shared? It might strengthen a relationship in ways you never expected. Those dollars you gave? They

could help someone find freedom in Jesus. The world says, "Protect what's yours." God invites you into a bolder way of living—one that defies conventional wisdom but aligns with His kingdom principles. In God's economy, nothing given in faith is ever truly lost.

Key Point

What you give in faith, God grows beyond what you can see.

Live It Out

- This week, when you feel the pull to hold back, choose one thing to share—your time, skill, or resource. Instead of focusing on the loss, pay attention to what happens next. How does it impact others? How does it change your own heart?

- Think back to a time when someone's generosity impacted your life. How did it shape your perspective? Share your story with a friend or your small group.

Prayer

> *Lord, when I'm tempted to hold onto what's mine, remind me that nothing given in faith is wasted. Help me trust that Your provision is greater than my fears. Teach me to give boldly, knowing that every small act of generosity ripples into eternity. Amen.*

Day 37
Growing Through Light and Dark

"Light is sweet, and it pleases the eyes to see the sun. However many years anyone may live, let them enjoy them all. But let them remember the days of darkness, for there will be many."

—Ecclesiastes 11:7–8

The warmth of the sun on your face. The golden glow of a sunset. Late-night conversations with friends that make time stand still. Some moments feel like pure light—undeniably good, effortlessly joyful.

But life isn't just highlight reels. Between those sun-filled moments stretch disappointments: failed tests, broken relationships, doubts about the future. The power lies not in avoiding these dark times, but in recognizing God's purposeful presence as you walk through them.

This balance of light and dark isn't just something to endure—it's actually the rhythm God designed for growth. Think about it: plants need both sunshine and rain. Muscles need both exercise and rest. Your faith needs both celebration and testing. Solomon, with all his wisdom and wealth, recognized this pattern as essential to a life well-lived.

"If I say, 'Surely the darkness will hide me and the light become night around me,' even the darkness will not be dark to you; the night will shine like the day, for darkness is as light to you" (Psalm 139:11–12).

Even when you can't see the purpose in your struggles, God sees clearly. The pain, confusion, and waiting seasons aren't wasted—they're shaping you. Your life right now is your training ground; each experience is an opportunity to develop deeper wisdom and stronger faith.

Key Point

God is just as present in your darkest days as He is in your brightest moments.

Live It Out

- Each day this week, record both a bright moment and a challenge. For each situation, write how you specifically recognized God's presence or what you learned. Look for patterns by the end of the week.

- Share your biggest insight with a friend who needs encouragement.

- Think about a time when God used a difficult season to prepare you for something important later. How did that experience change your perspective?

Prayer

Lord, thank You for walking with me through both bright and cloudy days. When life overflows with joy, help me embrace it fully. When darkness comes, remind me that You are near. Teach me to trust that You are working in every season and help me see the lessons You're growing within me. Amen.

Day 38
More Than Skin Deep

> *"So then, remove anxiety from your heart and cast off the troubles of your body, for youth and vigor are meaningless."*
>
> —**Ecclesiastes 11:10**

You pause mid-scroll. Another influencer flaunts a flawless body, effortlessly selling confidence. But instead of feeling inspired, a familiar pit settles in your stomach. You glance at your reflection, cataloging what doesn't measure up. Maybe if you worked out harder, ate cleaner, dressed differently—you'd finally feel *enough*.

Comparison keeps us perpetually unsatisfied. Just when you think you've caught up, the trends shift, the expectations rise, and the finish line moves further out of reach. Culture whispers that your worth is skin deep, but God tells a different story.

Like a high-performance car needs quality fuel and regular maintenance, your body isn't an ornament—it's an instrument designed for a greater purpose. Scripture reminds us: *"Do you not know that your bodies are temples of the Holy Spirit?"* (1 Corinthians 6:19). Taking care of yourself isn't about striving for an impossible ideal—it's about honoring the gift God has given you.

When exercise becomes about strength for service rather than sculpting for selfies, when nutrition becomes about fueling your purpose rather than fitting a profile, you find freedom from the anxiety Solomon warned about. The goal isn't perfection—it's stewardship of what God entrusted to you.

God sees you through the lens of love. Your body enables your dreams, empowers your passions, and reflects your incredible spirit. Whether it's worshiping with energy, serving others with strength, or creating with movement, your body was made for more than just display. While the world will always demand *more*—definition, beauty, perfection—your Creator declares you are already enough.

Key Point

Your body is an instrument for God's purpose, not a billboard for society's approval.

Live It Out

- This week, audit your social media:
  - Unfollow accounts that trigger unhealthy comparisons.
  - Follow people who encourage genuine health, confidence, and faith.
  - Talk with a trusted friend about how social influences affect your self-perception.
- Reflect on what God says about you—write down a Bible verse that speaks truth over your worth. Share this verse with someone who might need the same encouragement.

Prayer

Lord, help me see myself as You see me: loved, valuable, and wonderfully made. Free me from the anxiety of measuring up to impossible standards. Teach me to honor my body, not obsess over it, and embrace the purpose You designed me for. Amen.

Day 39
Right Here, Right Now

> *"Remember Him—before the silver cord is severed, and the golden bowl is broken; before the pitcher is shattered at the spring, and the wheel broken at the well … and the dust returns to the ground it came from, and the spirit returns to God who gave it."*
>
> **—Ecclesiastes 12:6–7**

Time feels infinite when you're young. Summer nights stretch on forever, and next year feels distant, as if there's always more time to figure things out. Life moves forward, but slowly—until one day, it doesn't.

Solomon's vivid imagery—a snapped lamp cord, a shattered pitcher, a broken water wheel—paints a striking picture: our bodies won't stay young forever. The dust we're made from will one day return to the earth. The question is: *What are we doing with the time we have right now?*

Every heartbeat is precious, every day an unrepeatable gift. Young as you are, you're already writing your story with the choices you make today.

Like a fresh journal waiting for your story, your journey with God is unfolding one page at a time. Some might say, "You have plenty of time," or "Just focus on having fun while you're young." But God whispers a different invitation: Don't wait.

"But grow in the grace and knowledge of our Lord and Savior Jesus Christ" (2 Peter 3:18).

This isn't about fearing the future. It's about embracing today. Every prayer whispered, every worship song that stirs your heart, every quiet moment in Scripture—these aren't just "someday" practices. They are the moments shaping who you're becoming. God isn't waiting for you to have it all figured out—He wants to meet you in the mess, in the questions, in the everyday moments that feel ordinary but are eternally significant.

Key Point

Your relationship with God isn't a "someday" thing—it's a right-now thing.

Live It Out

- This week, commit to one consistent daily moment with God:
    - Pick a time: During breakfast, on your commute, or before bed
    - Start small: Just five minutes in prayer or Scripture
    - Tell a friend: Share your plan so they can encourage you and keep you accountable

Prayer

Father, thank You that I don't have to wait to know You. Help me break free from distractions and make the most of today. Draw me closer, right now, just as I am. Teach me to see every moment as an opportunity to grow with You. Amen.

Day 40
Finding What Lasts

> *"Now all has been heard; here is the conclusion of the matter: Fear God and keep his commandments, for this is the duty of all mankind. For God will bring every deed into judgment, including every hidden thing, whether it is good or evil."*
>
> —Ecclesiastes 12:13–14

Imagine chasing every dream, experiencing every thrill, and achieving every goal—only to realize none of it fills the void inside. That was Solomon's reality. He had everything—riches beyond measure, wisdom admired by nations, pleasures without limit. Yet, the deeper he pursued the world's offerings, the emptier he became.

Like a ship lost at sea, trying every direction but never finding the shore, Solomon's search for fulfillment drifted through temporary pleasures, fleeting achievements, and human wisdom. But when he finally set his anchor in God, he discovered the only truth that lasts: **Life's deepest purpose is found in knowing and honoring God.**

"The fear of the Lord is the beginning of wisdom, and knowledge of the Holy One is understanding" (Proverbs 9:10). Solomon's final conclusion wasn't complicated—it was profoundly simple: **Revere God.** Obey Him. That's the foundation of a meaningful life.

We often overcomplicate purpose, chasing external success and cultural approval. But Solomon's wisdom reminds us:

- When God is your center, your choices carry eternal weight.
- When His wisdom guides you, your path becomes clear.
- When His love fuels your heart, even ordinary moments become sacred.

Every decision—whether standing for truth, resisting temptation, or influencing others—becomes an act of worship when your life is anchored in Him.

Key Point
Make God your life's true north—every choice finds meaning in Him.

Live It Out
- Take a moment to reflect on your entire forty-day journey. What has God revealed to you?
  - Identify the most significant decision you're currently facing—whether about relationships, career, faith, or integrity.
  - Write down how making the Lord your center influences this choice.
- Share your reflections with a mentor or trusted friend who can pray with you as you move forward in faith.

Prayer

> *Father, You are my anchor in a world of shifting desires. When distractions pull at my heart, remind me that true fulfillment is only found in You. Guide me through the decisions ahead, shaping my heart to want what You want. Help me follow You with confidence, even when the path feels uncertain. Thank You for walking with me every step of this journey. Amen.*

Deep Dive: Week 8 Review
Embracing Your Eternal Purpose

Everything in life eventually fades—success, wealth, and even the seasons we walk through. But what we do for God, how we love others, and our walk of faith will echo into eternity.

After wrestling with life's complexities, Solomon reaches this powerful conclusion: *"Fear God and keep his commandments, for this is the duty of all mankind"* (Ecclesiastes 12:13). Life, at its core, is about walking with God. With eternity in mind, our priorities shift, worries shrink, and daily choices gain deeper meaning.

Pause and Reflect

Living for what lasts means shifting from self-focus to God-focus, from temporary gain to eternal purpose.

1. What specific blessing or insight came from your act of giving this week?

2. Reflect on a moment of light and a moment of darkness. How did God meet you in both?

3. In what area of your life is God inviting you to trust Him more fully?

Creative Expression

Choose one way to capture your journey and how your perspective has grown through these eight weeks:

- Write about a moment when choosing God's way led to unexpected blessings.

- Create a simple drawing or collage showing your growth through these eight weeks.

- Tell a friend about one way this study has changed how you see your purpose.

Truth to Remember

Your true purpose isn't found in chasing achievement, but in walking daily with the God who created you for relationship with Him.

Looking Ahead

Completing this journey through Ecclesiastes is just the beginning. The next section will help you apply these discoveries to your daily life. As you move forward, ask yourself:

- How will I keep seeking God beyond this study?

- What practical steps can I take to live with eternal perspective every day?

Get ready—this next section will help you step into the future with wisdom, purpose, and confidence in God's plan.

Next Steps
Moving Forward with Purpose

Throughout these eight weeks, we've journeyed through many of life's deepest questions. We've explored what it means to find purpose beyond empty validation, discover authentic faith beyond performance, grow through both light and dark seasons, and build genuine connections in a world of surface relationships.

But what happens next? How do you take these insights and apply them to your daily life?

Ecclesiastes teaches that real meaning isn't found in perfectly crafted lives or endless achievements. It's found in knowing and walking with the One who created us for a purpose. As you close this devotional, remember: Every moment matters—not because it's social media-worthy, but because it's part of God's eternal plan for you.

Your growing pains, faith questions, struggles with comparison, and battles with temptation? They aren't wasted. Every challenge is shaping you, preparing you for what's ahead. When the path feels unclear, when heroes fall, or when answers aren't enough, remember: God meets you right where you are. The purpose you're seeking isn't found in achievements, likes, or others' opinions. It's found in walking daily with the God who designed you for more than surface living.

Practical Next Steps

Taking what you've learned and applying it to daily life is key. Here are some simple, intentional ways to keep growing:

- Find a trusted mentor or friend who will check in with you weekly about your spiritual growth. Choose someone who models the kind of authentic faith you want to develop.

- Schedule intentional time with God each day—disconnect from the noise and reconnect with Him. Try setting aside even ten minutes in the morning or before bed. Small, consistent moments create deep roots.

- Start a growth journal (digital or paper) to track your questions, victories, and insights. Writing things down helps you process your thoughts and recognize God's faithfulness over time.

- Pick a Bible reading plan that works for you. Use apps like YouVersion to start with short daily readings and build a sustainable habit.

- Join a small group or Bible study where you can share your journey with others. Faith grows stronger in community, and having people walk alongside you brings encouragement and accountability.

Share What You've Learned

If this devotional journey through Ecclesiastes has helped you grow, don't keep it to yourself! Share what you've learned—whether it's a favorite insight, a truth that transformed your thinking, or a moment that deepened your faith.

Tell a friend about the impact this study has had on you. Just as Solomon shared his wisdom, your story might be exactly what someone else needs to hear.

What's one truth from this study that changed how you see your purpose? Write it down. Then, take a step to live it out.

Final Prayer

> *Father, thank You for guiding me through these eight weeks. When I'm tempted to chase temporary satisfaction, draw me back to Your lasting purpose. Help me build genuine relationships, respond to authority with grace, and find strength in authentic community. Transform my surface-level faith into deep roots that can weather every season.*
>
> *Thank You that in Your hands, nothing is wasted. Even my struggles become stepping stones toward who You are shaping me to be. Guide me to use every gift, every challenge, and every opportunity to serve Your purpose. Help me live each day with an eternal perspective, knowing my life is part of something greater—Your plan.*
>
> *I trust You with my journey, Lord. Keep me walking in Your wisdom, growing in Your love, and living for what truly lasts. Amen.*

REQUEST

Was this book helpful? I'd love to hear from you!

Every review makes a difference!

Share how this devotional impacted your spiritual journey on Amazon or your favorite book platform.

Your comments help other readers discover this book and supports my work as an author.

Thanks in advance!

Lenora Trembath

About the Author

Lenora Trembath's journey to becoming an author was completely unexpected—until God opened a door she never saw coming. Her award-winning debut "The Wisdom Answer" launched her passion for making biblical wisdom relevant to modern challenges. Her own life's detours have equipped her to recognize the pitfalls that these principles help us avoid. As a former homeschool educator, she bridges timeless truth with everyday struggles.

When not writing, Lenora cherishes family time, especially playing card and board games. She is currently working on her next project.

www.ingramcontent.com/pod-product-compliance
Lightning Source LLC
Chambersburg PA
CBHW060506030426
42337CB00015B/1761